The AS 350/355 Book

Phil Croucher

About the Author

Phil Croucher holds JAR, UK, UAE, US and Canadian licences for aeroplanes and helicopters and around 8700 hours on 37 types, with a considerable operational background, and training experience from the computer industry. He is currently Head Of Training for Caledonian Advanced Pilot Training, the JAA licence conversion specialists (**www.captonline.com**).

Legal Bit

This book is sold as is without warranty of any kind, either express or implied, including but not limited to the implied warranties of merchantability and fitness for a particular purpose. Neither the Author, the Publisher nor their dealers or distributors assume liability for any alleged or actual damages arising from its use. **In other words**: *This book is for private study, and contains interpretations of official documentation, which changes, so there could be technical inaccuracies. As a result, alterations will be made without reference to anyone, and it's not guaranteed to suit your purposes. The author, publisher, and their distributors or dealers are not responsible for situations arising from its use.*

Any Manufacturer's Data information in their flight manuals is proprietary to Eurocopter. Disclosure, reproduction, or use of such data for any purpose other than helicopter operation is forbidden without prior written authorization from Eurocopter. The same goes for the content of this book!

Copyrights, etc.

All Rights Reserved

Praise for Professional Helicopter Pilot Studies:

"I wanted to take a few minutes and give you some feedback regarding your book "Professional Helicopter Pilot Studies". As a former Chief Pilot and Training Pilot I have gone through a lot of books over the years and have written quite a few of my own company handbooks and training courses. This is without a doubt the best book in its class.

Beyond the obvious fact that it is fantastic as a study manual, it is simply a pleasure to read. I found myself reading it for enjoyment as opposed to reading it simply to study. The typeface and layout are outstanding and a pleasure on the eyes. The copy flows nicely and is succinct without being dry; informative without being verbose.

Job well done!! I look forward to getting my hands on a few of your other books in the near future. Greg tells me that you're working on an ASTAR (Squirrel) handbook much like the Bell 206 one. I look forward to that. If that's the case I hope that you will include a robust section regarding the hydraulic system on the AS350. I've found over the years that most pilots have a very poor understanding of how the system actually works (which may have contributed to the various accidents in the past few years).

Warmest regards,"

Lee Johnson

"As far as the book goes, this is the best value I think anybody can have. I read through the Human Factors chapter, and HOLY COW! You got it right on. Best compilation over a relative few pages of so much material I have seen. Have read a few of these human factors books, and this chapter is stellar. You even used the same examples of accidents that I use, so it'll flow really good with my personal groundschool. I will use the Professional Pilot studies part for all the students, as well as CARs and the Helicopter Pilot's Handbook. This seems to give lots of value, without having to get another 10 pounds of wasted paper, in outdated books. Everything else is downloadable from Transport Canada!"

Harald Sydness, Chief Flight Instructor, Provincial Helicopters Ltd. FTU

Praise for The Helicopter Pilot's Handbook:

"a much needed summary of all the "basics" we live by. It sure is great for an old timer to see how all the things we had to find out the hard way in the 60's and 70's can now be found in a book. A great reference tool."

Robert Eschauzier

"A good insight into the working life of a pilot"

HF

"In short... great book! Thankfully your book illuminates many of the practical aspects of flying rotorcraft that are missing from the intro texts used during training. I'd equate much of the valuable practical information in your book to the to the same valuable information found in "Stick and Rudder."

Ian Campbell

"The chapters covering your experiences and showing 'the real world' of helicopter ops is a worthwhile addition to any pilots library and knowledge bank."

Paul

".....an excellent book for pilots interested in a career as a helicopter pilot. It answers all the really hard questions like "how does a young pilot get the required experience without having to join the army for 10 years". Great book for anyone interested in fling-wings!"

Reilly Burke, Technical Adviser, Aero Training Products

"Having only completed 20 hours of my CPL(H) in Australia, a lot of the content was very new to me. Your writing style is very clear and flowing, and the content was easy to understand. It's made me more eager than ever to finish my training and get into it. It's also opened my eyes as to how much there is to learn. The section on landing a job was excellent, especially for this industry that seems so hard to break into."

Philip Shelper

"Picked up The Helicopter Pilot's Handbook on Friday and have already read it twice. How you crammed that much very informative info into 178 pages is totally beyond me. WELL DONE. What a wealth of information, even though I only have a CPL-F. OUTSTANDING. I'm starting it again for the third time because I've picked up so much more the second time, that I'll read certainly a dozen more times. I cant wait to apply a lot the ideas and comments that you have supplied.

My wife is totally blown away that I've read it cover to cover twice and going around for a third time. She said it must be an outstanding book as I need real mental stimulus to keep me going.

Will

"I have only skimmed through the first version. Its already answered and confirmed a few things for me. Just the type of info I am after."

Andrew Harrison

".....provides many insights that wouldn't appear in the standard textbooks.

The next part of the book deals with the specialised tasks that a jobbing pilot may be called upon to do. It covers a very wide range of tasks from Avalanche Control through Ariel Photography and Filming; from Wildlife Capture to Winter Operations; from Pipeline Survey to Dropping Parachutists. This is not an exhaustive list of what he covers. If you need to know then it's probably here. The information given is good, practical and down to earth. It is exactly what you need to know and written from the pilot's point of view.

For anyone with some practical experience of helicopter operations it is worth a read. For someone who is going into civvie street and intends to fly then it is definitely worth a read. For anyone who intends to be a 'jobbing pilot' it could be invaluable as a source of reference."

Colin Morley
Army Air Corps

"Your book is very good and has been read by a few of the guys here with good 'raps'. particularly the Info on slinging etc. is stuff that is never covered in endorsement training. Certainly a worthwhile addition to any pilot library."

Gibbo

UNITED KINGDOM CIVIL AVIATION AUTHORITY

Member of the Joint Aviation Authorities

APPROVAL CERTIFICATE

This certificate is issued to:

CALEDONIAN ADVANCED PILOT TRAINING LIMITED

Number **UK/FTO-310**

THE CIVIL AVIATION AUTHORITY, pursuant to the powers contained in Article 77(a) of the Air Navigation Order 2009 confirms that the above named organisation complies in all respects with the Joint Aviation Requirements (JAR-FCL) relating to the establishment of a Training Organisation and is empowered to operate as an approved Flight Training Organisation for the courses listed in the attached Schedule.

The Courses shall be conducted at the following training centres:

WADLEY COURT, CHAPEL STREET, BICESTER AND WEST PALM BEACH, FLORIDA, USA

The Head of Training under whose direction the Course shall be conducted shall be **CAPTAIN P CROUCHER**

This certificate, unless cancelled, suspended or revoked shall continue in effect until **31 OCTOBER 2014**

Date of issue: 23 August 2011

Signature

For Civil Aviation Authority

TRAINING APPROVAL SCHEDULE
Organisation: Caledonian Advanced Pilot Training Limited
Approval Number: UK/FTO-310

Centre	Course
Wadley Court Chapel Street Bicester OX26 6BD	ATPL (Aeroplanes) Modular Theoretical Knowledge (Distance-Learning) ATPL (Helicopters) Modular Theoretical Knowledge (Distance-Learning) CPL (Helicopters) Modular Theoretical Knowledge (Distance-Learning) Single Pilot Multi-Engine (Helicopters) Modular Pre-Entry Theoretical Knowledge (Distance-Learning) IR (Helicopters) Modular Theoretical Knowledge (Distance-Learning) Military Bridging Modular Theoretical Knowledge (Distance-Learning) Aeroplane To Helicopter Bridging Modular Theoretical Knowledge (Distance-Learning)
Cloud 9 Helicopters 11610 Aviation Blvd West Palm Beach Florida 33412 United States	ATPL (Aeroplanes) Modular Theoretical Knowledge (Distance-Learning) ATPL (Helicopters) Modular Theoretical Knowledge (Distance-Learning)

Date of issue: 23 August 2011

Signature

For Civil Aviation Authority

Contents

CONTENTS

INTRODUCTION

T his book is not intended to be a replacement for the flight manual, or a substitute for a proper conversion course, but a training aid for people coming to the AS 350 for the first time, or pilots who have been flying it for years who would like to know more about how it really works. A lot of knowledge about how helicopters work is therefore assumed, and only mentioned when it makes understanding the machine easier. Similarly, stuff that is better left in the flight manual remains there.

Suggested checklists are included for Commercial Air Transport operations.

THE BASICS

The Astar, or Squirrel, depending on which side of the Atlantic you're on, carries 6 people, including the pilot. It comes in several flavours.

It was originally designed as a replacement for the Alouette II, and came out as an Aerospatiale machine in the first instance. It is now made by Eurocopter. It first flew on June 26th 1974 and came into production in 1975.

The original was the B (whatever happened to the A?), running through the BA, B1, B2, B3 and C to the D, which is just a B with a Lycoming engine which, unfortunately, did not win much respect in the early days - the book containing the ADs alone would make you overweight. OK, so I'm exaggerating, but it is big. The engine was originally designed for the M-1 tank, but also got used in the Canadair Challenger, BAE 146, Bell 222, BK-117, and possibly the HH-65.

This success hadn't been anticipated, and when it started to have problems, they were told that the Army had priority, based on the fact they owned the factory they were being made in, which meant that all the other installations suffered. These days, only minor problems remain.

The DA is the BA with the same engine, and the Super D has the latest model (that is, it is a BA with the modern LTS 101). The C was the first with a LTS 101 600A and was actually type certified before the B. The D came later with the LTS 101 600A2 (the SD1 is a BA/B1 with a -600 and an SD2 is a B2 with a -700).

Cs and Ds are not officially supported by Eurocopter - in fact, the French authorities pulled the certificate for the C model in 1997. The D, however, is still very much alive, and those who operate them alongside Bs report that the D with the later LTS 101 is easier on fuel, easier to start, more reliable and has much lower direct operating costs (and probably less down time while waiting for a replacement engine). In fact, the engine can be operated "on condition", and you can do a lot on the Lycoming with local engineers.

According to Honeywell, the LTS101-700D2 is designed to the same power level as the original Arriel 1D1, but with improved specific fuel consumption and reliability due to a new, cooled gas producer turbine that improves the disk life from 6,500 to 15,000 cycles, and an updated reduction gear from other LTS101 models. These changes reduce power turbine cycles by 35% and increase torque limits by 6%.

The LTS101-700D2 apparently gives the AS 350 SD2 a 14% increase in sea-level standard day takeoff power (18% when hot and high compared to the LTS101-600A-3A in a previous Soloy conversion of the AS 350B2.

The D1 is the same as the D, but with a lower MTOW. There is a Super D with an LTS 101 750 and B2 running gear, and an attempt by Soloy to install an Allison 250C30, as found on the Bell 206L.

The BB is a UK military training aircraft (HT1 for the RAF, and HT2 for the Army) which is possibly a BA with a 1D1 in it, and a geared hydraulic pump instead of one driven by a belt (why couldn't they do that in the first place?) Other military versions include the L, L1 (B1) and L2 (B2), but if I told you about them I would have to kill you.

The HB 350 and HB 355 are just versions produced by Helibras in Brazil (as the Esquilo, for their military). They are identical to the Eurocopter versions.

Along with the B, which has the Arriel 1B engine, the C and D models have blue MR Blades.

In summary:

- The **BA** is a B with grey main rotor blades and tail rotor blades from the 355, plus a few modifications to the transmission deck.

- The **B1** is a BA with an Arriel 1D engine and TR compensator and boom strake.

- The **B2** adds an Arriel 1D1 and different tailpipe.

- The **B3** is a B2 with an Arriel 2 engine (FADEC) VEMD and no tail boom strake as it has the 355N's tail rotor. It was designed to replace the Llama as a high-altitude lifter. There is a special B3e version with an Arriel 2D engine.

- The **B4** (EC 130) is an EC120 at the front, a B3 in the middle (with dual hydraulics) and an EC135 in the tail, albeit a mirror image due to the direction of rotation. Essentially, the B3's fuselage structure was widened, and a new fibreglass canopy was made over the top.

The blades on the B2 and B3 have the same dimensions and profile but the B3 blade's spar is a lot stiffer to accommodate the increased gross weight.

Otherwise, the essential difference between all AS 350s is the increase in power and payload with each step, and the engines, of course (the gross weight limitations mainly concern controllability without hydraulics. The B3 has the worst useful load internally due to this restriction).

All except the B (which has blue blades) share the same airframe and main and tail rotor arrangements as the Twinstar, which itself comes in three flavours, the F1 and F2, with Allison engines, as per the Bell 206, and the N, which has the same engines as the EC120 and 135, the Arrius. Disc loading is therefore most on the B, as the blades have a smaller chord to carry 4300 lbs (Twinstar blades have an asymmetrical chord and a 2 inch wider span, from 11.7 to 13.7 ins).

The B3 has a FADEC and the *Vehicle and Engine Multifunction Display* (VEMD), which is a twin-glass panel that shows engine power limitations, turbine temperatures and torque limitations as a single numeric reading from 1-10. When the needle goes into the red zone at 10, regardless of which parameter is exceeded, an aural warning tells you to reduce power. However, all three parameters are shown in digital form down the side - when the alarm goes off, the system being exceeded is first underlined in yellow as a warning, then red as an alert. As well, after you enter the empty weight, crew weight and payload, it can read the fuel weight and OAT, then compute maximum HIGE and HOGE weights.

Operation

The AS 350 is approved for Day or Night VFR non-icing conditions, according to State regulations, and assuming the right equipment. It can carry a lot more than the 206L, with plenty of power and tail rotor authority, which allows you to hover OGE in almost any wind without trouble, so it's quite effective for mountain flying (although, when you get really high up, the N_G will top out first, with a good chance of compressor blade creep if you overspeed).

It's very cyclic-sensitive, with the rear right skid hanging much lower than the 206's left skid in the hover, where it positively dances, probably due to how the downwash interacts with the tail rotor.

For example, when OGE, the main rotor wake misses the tail rotor completely. When IGE, it can be in and out of the wake according to the wind direction. As it can obtain translational lift by itself, the tail rotor thrust can vary continually, and a yaw/roll coupling can be induced. People tend to try and counteract it with the cyclic, which is a natural reaction, but the wrong one. Keep the machine straight with good footwork.

It became much better when they installed the long tailpipe on the exhaust on the B3, as it did on the 355 with the trailing edge tab on the blade.

The machine overall demands a light touch to fly properly, even though it has a much greater all-up weight, so don't grip the controls or push your feet against the pedals too much!

> *"enjoy the A/C but learn your product well....... although a nimble and responsive A/c it should be flown more like a medium. If you have a penchant for being a cowboy - leave the boots and spurs at home on this one. This is not meant to frighten, however knowledge is one of the gateways to professionalism."*

Initially, at least, the best way to take off and land is to behave as if you are on sloping ground.

The cargo swing can damage the belly when landing in snow, and the fuel sump drain can also be activated. Ice on the bottom of the skids can reduce the effect of the stinger (the heel spring on the rear of the skid that reduces the tendency for ground resonance), and ice can cause problems in the tail rotor system hydraulics.

The visibility for slinging is not so good, which has led to a modification in the shape of a window in the floor panel, and you often need a longer line than normal just to see the load (at least 100 ft).

However, the visibility for other work, such as power line inspection, is not bad at all (though not as good as the 206):

THE AIRFRAME

The fuselage is split into three components, the forward, intermediate and tail sections. Measurements, etc., are in the *Data* section.

The picture below shows the materials used in its construction. The machine shown is the 355, but the 350 is almost identical - effectively just replace titanium with steel and swap a couple of the windscreen plastics.

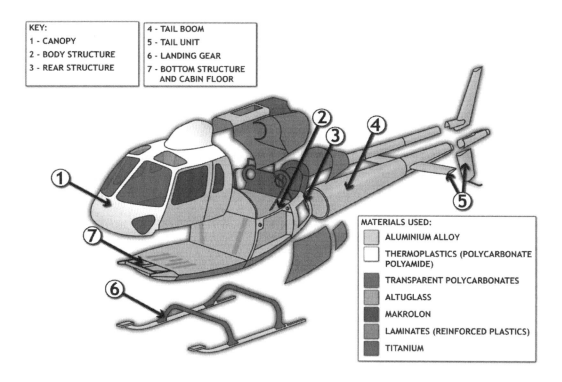

KEY:
1 - CANOPY
2 - BODY STRUCTURE
3 - REAR STRUCTURE
4 - TAIL BOOM
5 - TAIL UNIT
6 - LANDING GEAR
7 - BOTTOM STRUCTURE AND CABIN FLOOR

MATERIALS USED:
- ALUMINIUM ALLOY
- THERMOPLASTICS (POLYCARBONATE POLYAMIDE)
- TRANSPARENT POLYCARBONATES
- ALTUGLASS
- MAKROLON
- LAMINATES (REINFORCED PLASTICS)
- TITANIUM

The one-piece windscreen is made of Lexan, a polycarbonate (the two-piece is plexiglass). Both types require special cleaning.

The cabin is also constructed of polycarbonate (80%), with glass fibre (20%), which is supposed to be stronger than aluminium. However, it provides a minimal amount of protection, since the strength-bearing part of the fuselage is the cantilever which supports the cabin as an extension of the body structure (having said that, people have been known to walk away from crashes where the cabin has been destroyed).

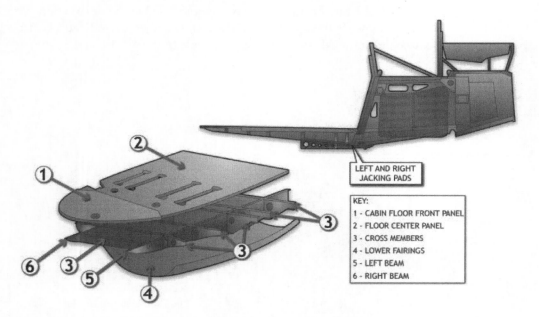

LEFT AND RIGHT
JACKING PADS

KEY:
1 - CABIN FLOOR FRONT PANEL
2 - FLOOR CENTER PANEL
3 - CROSS MEMBERS
4 - LOWER FAIRINGS
5 - LEFT BEAM
6 - RIGHT BEAM

A cantilever is a beam supported at one end. In the 350, two beams, stiffened with cross beams, are riveted to the body structure side beams to support the forward section of the landing gear.

Note: The windscreen is an integral part of the cabin structure. When installing the panels, the screws must be tightened in a particular sequence to avoid introducing stresses in the assembly.

There are two main classes of synthetic resin used:

- **Thermoplastics**, which soften when heated and *vice versa*. For example, polyamides (Nylon, Rilsan) and polycarbonates

- **Thermosetting resins**, which, with heat and a hardener, cure when heated, and stay that way as a new material (epoxy resin, etc.)

Laminated materials are produced from thermosetting resins and reinforcing materials, such as carbon fibres, which are laid out as a mat or in woven form (the direction depends on the loads to be transmitted), then impregnated with the basic resin. Several layers are stacked, placed in a mould and cured.

Laminated honeycombs have a core made on metal, glasscloth or Nomex^{TM}, each face of which goes against one or more impregnated layers. The assembly is then oven cured. An example is shown below:

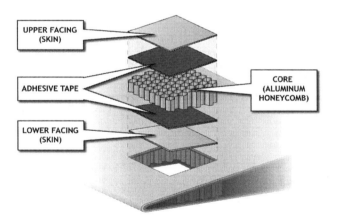

STRUCTURE

• •

The Body

This is the strongest part of the airframe, as it directly supports flight and landing loads.

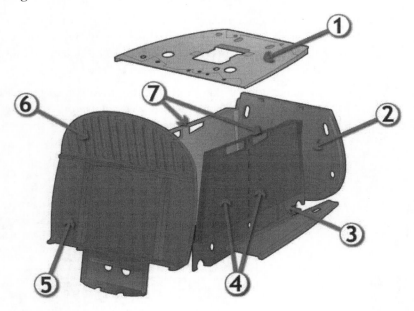

KEY:

1 - TRANSMISSION PLATFORM

2 - REAR BULKHEAD (ATTACHMENT OF REAR STRUCTURE)

3 - LATERAL BEAMS (LEFT AND RIGHT SIDES)

4 - STRUCTURAL FUEL TANKS

5 - FRONT BULKHEAD (TILTED 15° REARWARD)

6 - UPPER BULKHEAD (TILTED 7° FORWARD)

7 - LONGITUDINAL BULKHEADS (THICK PLATES)

It is designed as a rigid box (hexaedron), which supports the main gearbox and rotors, landing gear and the rear structure, plus the fuel tank inside.

Canopy

The canopy includes the cabin roof, the nose and vertical members.

1 - NOSE
2 - VERTICAL MEMBERS (3)
3 - REAR STRUCTURE

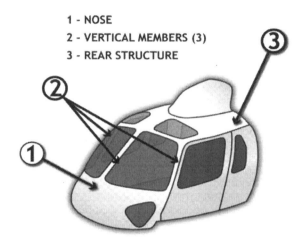

The components are made from glass-reinforced polycarbonate (80%) and reinforced with fibreglass (20%), heat moulded and assembled by bending and ultrasonic spot welding. The canopy frame is bolted to the cabin floor and body structure bulkhead.

The roof is a pair of half shells which have cabin air ducted inside them.

There is a sideslip indicator (a piece of wool) on the outside of the vertical member, just above the pitot tube(s).

DOORS

There are two cabin doors, one on either side, that give access to the pilot seats. Behind each one there is a smaller door for the rear section of the cabin. Normally, the doors are not jettisonable, but there is an optional system that allows it.

The pilot doors have a compressed air expansion arm that helps the door open and keeps it open (air is compressed when the door is closed).

All doors can be removed, but flight with only one removed on each side is not approved, except for the (optional) sliding door.

Tip: When closing, push on the back of the front door 20 cm up from the bottom. Higher up (near the handle) causes it to distort and be difficult.

The baggage and rear compartment doors are made of laminate. Those on the baggage compartment are hinged at the top and can be held open by a rod that clips inside the door when it is not being used. They also have two locks each that control microswitches (in parallel) that illuminate a warning light on the caution panel when they are not engaged.

The rear baggage compartment should not be filled too much, as the tail rotor controls may be restricted (they live just above it). There is an electrical panel behind it, too, which is a prime target for leaks from the baggage compartment.

Rear Structure

This consists of three frames (3, 5, and 9 in the picture) connected by beams. The engine is supported by the rear and forward ones. The tail boom is bolted to the junction frame (3). There is a baggage compartment inside.

KEY:

1 - ENGINE DECK (STAINLESS STEEL PLATE)

2 - BEAM UNDER ENGINE DECK

3 - JUNCTION FRAME (SUPPORTS REAR JACKING ADAPTER)

4 - SKIN

5 - REAR FRAME

6 - ACCESS TO BAGGAGE COMPARTMENT

7 - RECESS (FOOTSTEP FOR ACCESS TO TRANSMISSION PLATFORM)

8 - BAGGAGE COMPARTMENT FLOOR (ACCESS TO ELECTRICAL MASTER UNITS)

9 - FORWARD FRAME

10 - ENGINE MOUNTING BEAMS

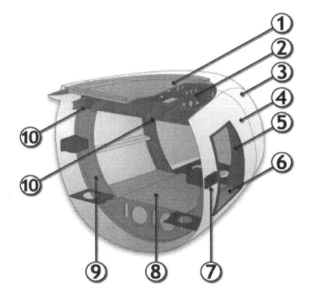

The Tail Boom

The tail boom is monocoque, with circular frames covered by an outer skin. Sheet metal stiffeners between the frames ensure that it stays rigid. It supports the following items:

- The tail rotor gearbox (on a reinforced frame)

- The horizontal stabiliser (between two reinforced frames)

- The tail rotor drive shafts

- The vertical fins

Ballast weights can be fitted inside the tail cone to correct the C of G position, when you have something large (like a movie camera) mounted in front of the nose, or lots of instruments in the front (you can actually have the battery moved to the tail boom to save you doing it).

The tail unit includes a horizontal stabiliser, and an upper and lower vertical fin, which is protected by a tail skid in case of a nose-high landing.

The stabiliser and fins are aerofoils that can keep the aircraft straight and provide some sort of stability by bringing it back to its initial attitude if it is affected by gusts or other disturbances.

Note: The stabilising function only works above a certain minimum airspeed (V_{TOSS}).

THE HORIZONTAL STABILISER

This has an asymmetric NACA profile that create a downward force in flight to stop any nose-down tendency.

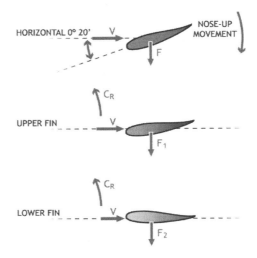

THE FINS

In the cruise, the asymmetric NACA profile of the upper fin opposes the main rotor torque, acting in the same direction as tail rotor thrust. This reduces the tail rotor pitch and hence the power required.

The lower fin is symmetrical, also with a NACA profile, which generates a force in the same direction as the upper fin.

Notice the difference in angles between the two in the picture on the right:

The vertical fins on some models have different arrangements of Gurney flaps to improve directional stability. This is a small flat tab that projects from the trailing edge of an aerofoil, usually at a right angle to the pressure side surface, at

1 - 2% of the wing chord. This can improve the performance of a simple aerofoil markedly. It works by increasing pressure on the pressure side, decreasing pressure on the suction side, and helping the boundary layer flow stay attached all the way to the trailing edge on the suction side.

More technically, the Gurney flap increases the maximum lift coefficient (C_{Lmax}), decreases the angle of attack for zero lift, and increases the nose-down pitching moment, which is in line with an increase in camber. It also typically increases the drag coefficient (C_D), especially at low angles of attack, although for thick aerofoils, a reduction in drag has been reported. In short, the increased pressure on the lower surface ahead of the flap means the upper surface suction can be reduced while producing the same lift over a very wide range of positive and negative angles of attack.

The AS 355 uses a double Gurney flap that projects from both surfaces of the vertical stabilizer. It corrects a problem with lift reversal in thick airfoil sections at low angles of attack. The double gurney flap reduces the control input required to transition from hover to forward flight.

STRAKES (B2)

In sideways flight to the left, the main rotor downwash is deflected and accelerated over the right hand side of the tail boom (looking forward), which can introduce a negative pressure of around 1 mb along it, which reduces the effect of the tail rotor, typically by about 5%. A strake added at 45° makes the downwash flow separate and restore the lost pressure.

This, of course, increases the tail rotor's efficiency.

The strake, therefore, is designed to generate a pressure equal to the static pressure on the relevant side of the tail boom.

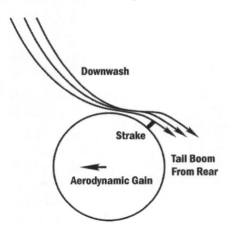

© *Phil Croucher, 2011*

Landing Gear

The landing gear supports the aircraft, protects the structure on landing and dampens vibrations on the ground when the rotors are turning.

It consists of two aluminium alloy skids, two steel cross tubes, and two hydraulic shock absorbers.

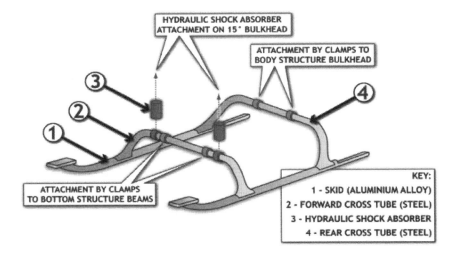

HYDRAULIC SHOCK ABSORBER ATTACHMENT ON 15° BULKHEAD

ATTACHMENT BY CLAMPS TO BODY STRUCTURE BULKHEAD

ATTACHMENT BY CLAMPS TO BOTTOM STRUCTURE BEAMS

KEY:
1 - SKID (ALUMINIUM ALLOY)
2 - FORWARD CROSS TUBE (STEEL)
3 - HYDRAULIC SHOCK ABSORBER
4 - REAR CROSS TUBE (STEEL)

In flight, the assorted rotors, engine(s) and drive shafts transmit their own vibrations to the structure which are generally stabilised because there is no real focal point for them to attach to.

On the ground, however, with the rotors turning, they can focus through the landing gear. When the gear's natural frequency matches that of the main rotor, other reflected pulses are received, which markedly increase the amplitude of the vibrations, to create ground resonance.

There is a flexible steel strip that is bent downwards at the rear of the skids that increases the gear's flexibility and changes its natural frequency so that ground resonance should not occur*. The shock absorbers do their bit by absorbing the vibrations and eliminating divergent oscillations.

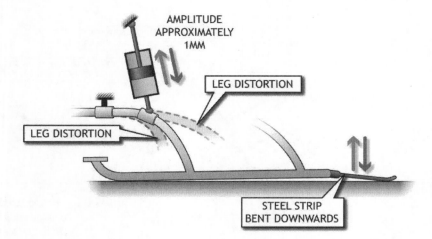

*Assuming the steel-spring extensions are precisely in place. The design is not immune to ground resonance if they are slightly off.

© *Phil Croucher, 2011*

THE COCKPIT

The cockpit layout is fairly standard.

Note: Console switches are NEVER the same between machines. Always read them before using them!

This is an example of what they should look like.

EXT PWR BATT	FUEL PUMP 1	GENE	GENE RESET	CRANK	MASTER SW
W/LT TEST	FUEL PUMP 2	A/COL LT	POS LTS	HYDR TEST	HORN
PITOT	INST LTS 1	INST LTS 2	STROB LIGHT	TAXI LIGHT	LAND LIGHT
STANDBY HORIZON	FLOW METER	SAND FILTER	LS	CONF	W/S WIPER
INVERT	ATTITUDE	GYRO COMPASS	TRIM RELEASE	PITCH TRIM ACTUATOR	ROLL TRIM ACTUATOR
FLOAT ARM	SLING	HOISTL	FLARE	SPARE	FLOAT FIRING

Cabin Heating

This comes out from under the pilot's seats, having been tapped from Station 2 of the Arriel compressor, or Station 3 of the LTS 101. The P2 or P3 air is mixed with ambient (through a venturi tube) air to create the desired temperature.

VEMD

The Vehicle and Engine Multifunction Display replaces many conventional instruments and lives in the centre of the instrument panel of the B3, when fitted.

The system consists of 2 processor modules and a display module, which has two Active Matrix LCDs:

Down the side is a series of 10 buttons that control the displays and their functions.

Both processors receive the same data, and compare them. Any differences will cause an error message to be displayed. If one fails, the other is able to perform by itself.

The **OFF1** and **OFF2** buttons turn the upper and lower displays on and off, respectively, together with their associated processors.

On power-up and after the self-test, the VEMD displays three parameters in its upper screen - T4.5, N_1 and torque. When N_1 exceeds 60%, however, it switches to the First Limit Indicator display, as shown above.

Pressing **SCROLL** twice displays a performance page, in which the +, - and **ENTER** keys can be used to record the payload. The VEMD can compute the AUW and the maximum takeoff weights IGE or OGE. At the end of the flight, it can also produce a flight report that includes the flight time, the generator and turbine cycles and any overlimits or failures that occurred during the flight.

FLYING CONTROLS

The swashplate is operated by three mobile cylinder servo controls (two lateral, one fore-and-aft).

Control movements are transmitted to the starflex, which bends to control rotor pitch.

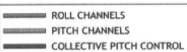

ROLL CHANNELS
PITCH CHANNELS
COLLECTIVE PITCH CONTROL

1 · RH ROLL SERVO-CONTROL
2 · PITCH SERVO-CONTROL
3 · SWASHPLATE
4 · LH ROLL SERVO-CONTROL
5 · MIXING UNIT
6 · COPILOT'S COLLECTIVE PITCH LEVER (QUICK-REMOVAL, DUAL CONTROL)
7 · COLLECTIVE LEVER TORQUE SHAFT
8 · COPILOT'S CYCLIC STICK (QUICK-REMOVAL, DUAL CONTROL)
9 · CYCLIC STICK TORQUE SHAFT
10 · LATERAL CYCLIC BELLCRANK
11 · PILOT'S CYCLIC STICK
12 · PILOT'S COLLECTIVE LEVER
13 · CYCLIC CHANNEL INTERMEDIATE LEVERS
14 · COLLECTIVE PITCH/ENGINE GOVERNOR COUPLING
15 · SERVO-CONTROL INPUT RODS

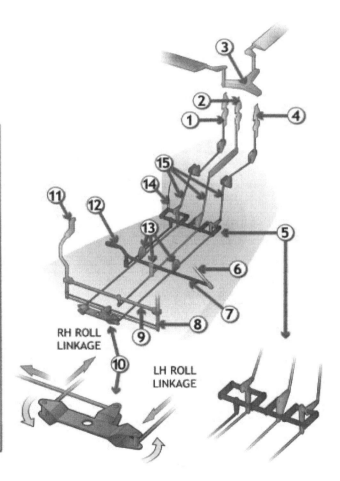

RH ROLL LINKAGE

LH ROLL LINKAGE

Control Mixing

In helicopters that have their collective pitch changed by moving the whole swashplate up and down the rotor mast, there must be some way of making sure that the cyclic is not affected. Otherwise, moving the collective would alter the height of the cyclic setting on the swashplate, and alter the disc attitude. Moving the cyclic would also screw with the collective.

A *mixing unit* maintains the cyclic angle by superimposing collective inputs onto cyclic inputs, keeping the disc angle constant. It consists of a series of summing bellcranks and torque tubes.

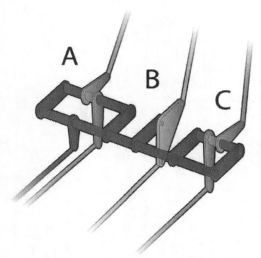

Upward movement of the collective moves the swashplate as well, and the cyclic input that was already there moves the same amount in the same direction. In the picture above, cranks A, B and C all move at the same time.

When fore and aft cyclic is used, however, only crank B moves upwards to tilt the swashplate in the desired direction. Lateral movements will move only A & C in equal and opposite directions.

© *Phil Croucher, 2011*

The Engine

T The powerplant is mounted inside a fireproof compartment and linked to the main gearbox at the forward end through a flared coupling casing, as described in the *Transmission* section. At the rear end, it is attached to the platform with two rubber anti-vibration mounts.

The AS 350 officially comes with an Arriel engine, as described here, but there may also be an LTS engine, not mentioned all that much.

Both weigh 109 kg, and are free turbines, which use a governor system to keep the free turbine at a constant RPM at any value of collective pitch. This means that the gas generator RPM may vary*, and that the power delivered to the rotors depends only on engine torque.

*The gas generator and power turbine shafts are completely independent.

The engines have no clutch on the drive shaft. They have a modular design and an integral freewheel.

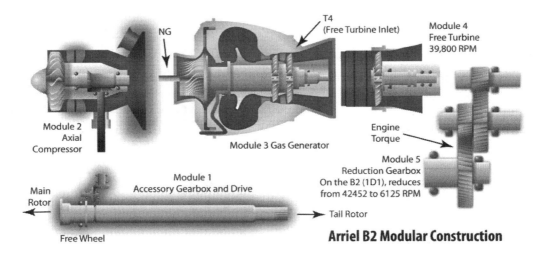

Arriel B2 Modular Construction

Note: As the AS350 is not typically flown by low-time pilots, you should refer to my Professional Helicopter Study books for basic gas turbine operation.

ARRIEL ENGINE

GAS GENERATOR

FREE TURBINE SPEED CONSTANT: AT 39,800 RPM

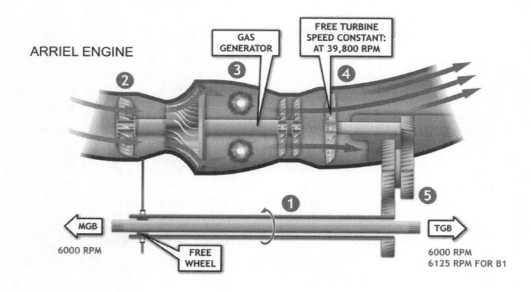

MGB
6000 RPM

FREE WHEEL

TGB
6000 RPM
6125 RPM FOR B1

LTS ENGINE

GAS GENERATOR

FREE TURBINE SPEED CONSTANT: AT 37,000 RPM

REDUCTION GEAR

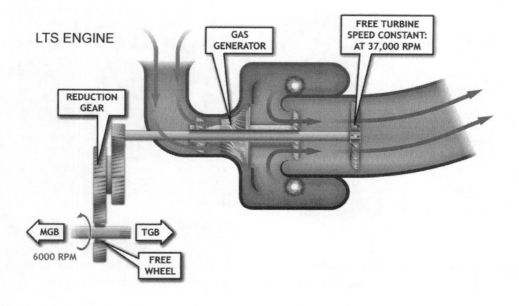

MGB
6000 RPM

TGB

FREE WHEEL

ARRIEL

The Arriel family has a single-stage axial and a centrifugal compressor, an annular combustion chamber with centrifugal fuel injection and ignition, a two-stage axial turbine to drive the compressors and a single-stage free power turbine. It has self-contained lubrication with external oil cooling system and oil tank.

A letter relates the engine to the version of the helicopter it is in.

	Engine	*Rotor*	*T/O Wt*	*T/O Pwr*	*Max Cont*	*Rotor Speed*
B	Arriel 1B	350	1950 kg	478 KW	440 KW	385 RPM +1 -4
BA	Arriel 1B	355	2100 kg	478 KW	440 KW	390 RPM +4 -5
B1	Arriel 1D	355	2200 kg	510 KW	450 KW	390 RPM +4 -5
B2	Arriel 1D1	355	2250 kg	531 KW	466 KW	390 RPM +4 -5
B3	Arriel 2B	355	2250 kg	632 KW	543 KW	390 RPM +4 -5
B3	Arriel 2B1	355	2250 kg	632 KW	543 KW	375-405 RPM

The engine's bearings and gears are lubricated and cooled by circulating oil under pressure. It is hot when it comes out of the engine and, to preserve its lubricating qualities, must be cooled, so monitoring the condition of the oil is important. The parameters concerned are temperature and pressure, which usually vary inversely with each other - as oil temperature increases, its pressure decreases.

After lubricating the engine, the hot oil is sucked up by scavenge pumps and fed to the cooling system, which is in the airflow*. A new cycle starts when oil is drawn from the tank by a pressure pump and into the engine.

During starting, the oil is heated up quickly with the help of a thermostat valve, which is open when the temperature is below 74°C, so the oil returns directly to the tank. At 74°C and above, the valve progressively closes, and it is fully closed at 86°C, making the oil flow through the cooler (this is the normal situation when the engine is hot).

*In the hover, cooling air is generated by a motor-driven fan which starts when the oil temperature in the tank reaches 77°C. It stops when the oil temperature drops below 68°C.

Longer rundowns on the Arriel are not good for it. The temperature in the bearings initially goes down but after 30 secs it goes all over the place. The problem is low oil flow at idle. In fact if you do idle an Arriel it is better to run it back to **FLIGHT** for a period before shutting it down.

The injection wheel is subject to considerable thermal cycle fatigue. If it fails, most of the gas generator rotating assembly will leave the engine rapidly.

Picture: Arriel Engine

© *Phil Croucher, 2011*

Starting

There are two mechanical controls to the engine, on the floor between the seats. Many operators have them guarded to stop inadvertent closing of the throttle by passenger camera straps, etc.

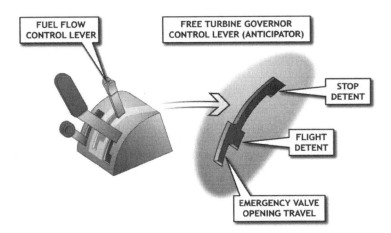

FUEL FLOW CONTROL LEVER

FREE TURBINE GOVERNOR CONTROL LEVER (ANTICIPATOR)

STOP DETENT

FLIGHT DETENT

EMERGENCY VALVE OPENING TRAVEL

The fuel flow control lever operates two flow control valves. In the first part of its travel (from the **STOP** to the **FLIGHT** detents) it progressively opens the main valve. In the second part, beyond the **FLIGHT** detent, it opens the emergency control valve, which is there to supply the engine if the governing system fails. When it is fully back, both valves are closed.

Air and high energy sparks (for the ignition) are supplied when you push the start button on top of the fuel flow control lever. Fuel is supplied when the lever is moved forwards into the starting range. When it is there, the main valve is partly opened and the bleed valve is closed.

Note: The starter will not operate with the rotor brake on, or not locked OFF! Check this first before you call an engineer!

Tip: Place the little finger of your left hand on the throttle quadrant when adding fuel during the start. This makes your hand steadier and you will get much finer control (and fewer T4 excursions).

You then adjust the fuel flow delivered to the injectors by opening the flow valve to keep the T4 within limits.

If the N_G hangs at 15%, carefully push the throttle forward in small increments (3-4) while closely monitoring the T4 (there will be a lag between throttle movement and T4 rise).

Once ignited, the fuel/air mixture supplies the energy which, added to that from the starter, accelerates the engine, so fuel and airflow both increase until the engine reaches self-sustaining speed. At this point the button is released and the starter and igniters stop working.

The fuel flow lever is moved forward to the **FLIGHT** position where the main valve is fully open and the governing system takes over. Torque should not normally exceed 30% when doing this.

Some models, such as the B3, have a twist grip throttle on the collective instead of the throttle lever on the floor. In fact, the B3 has 3 different types:

- The first had a thumb lock release switch to increase the throttle setting in manual governor (**MAN GOV**) range

- The second had a automatic release of the override lock when operating in **MAN GOV**

- The latest version just has an idle to full open throttle setting, with no **MAN GOV** switch. The start switch in the roof now has only the **OFF** & **FLIGHT** settings

Fuel Control

The free turbine governor's job is to keep the speed of the free turbine (and rotor blades) constant, irrespective of the fuel flow and power demands.

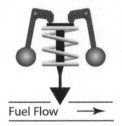

Fuel Flow →

Although the governor detects RPM variations and issues control orders, it doesn't get much feedback, so the rotor RPM is not always constant in the true sense of the word - it will drop slightly as power is increased and rise when power demands decrease. This slight difference in RPM is called static droop, and it can occur whenever a flyweight centrifugal governor is used on a free turbine engine. Its value depends on the spring tension (the pitch/governor coupling).

The free turbine drives flyweights which fly outwards as engine RPM is increased, which compresses a spring that pushes a needle into the fuel flow to restrict its movement through the hole. If, at a stabilised RPM, RRPM decreases (say after an increase in collective pitch), the centrifugal force decreases and the spring will move the flyweights closer in to each other. This will pull the needle out of the hole and allow more fuel through to increase the rotor RPM.

In the LTS engine, the Power Turbine Governor senses and controls the N_2/RRPM by modifying air pressures within the FCU. It's not far removed from that on the Bell 206L, being a modulated Bendix system.

FADEC

The initials stand for *Full Authority Digital Electronic Control*. It's just a computer that controls the fuel system (like an electronic FCU), based on information from various sensors, such as exhaust temperature, engine RPM, control movement, etc. (typical inputs are TOT and N_1).

The end result is a more precise control of rotor speeds under varying flight conditions, particularly for overspeeding. Other benefits include automatic starting, optimal fuel metering, faster response to power demands, better care of the engine (more time between overhauls) and reduction of pilot workload through automation. It is also better at limiting. Being a computer, it is software-based, and one preflight check is to ensure that the right software is loaded. Also, as it's a computer, it can monitor many parameters, which is why you might see more caution lights.

A FADEC has the following functions:

- Flow regulation
- Automatic starting sequence
- Transmission of engine data to pilot's instruments
- Thrust management and protection of limits
- Prevent overtemperature or overspeed

The B3 and B4 both use a FADEC although the B3's is single channel (the newer ones are dual channel, as with the B4).

The FADEC uses OAT to set a basic fuel flow, which it adjusts to get a certain T4 for a certain N_1 speed.

Note: This does not necessarily automatically handle a hot start! However, with the new TU standard DECU software (TU143 for the single channel and TU144 for the dual channel) it will automatically abort the start by closing the electro valve if the T4 reaches 865°.

People transitioning from other machines may be used to cranking an engine over before starting to reduce the temperature (usually to below 150°). The Arriel engine (and the Arrius) both inject fuel right away. That is, they don't spool up to a 15% before fuel is introduced as with the Bell 206, for example. Below about 10% N_1 the only fuel going into the engine should be through the injectors, which will only supply enough to get about 200-300° T4, so if you are at only 200°, you should be able to start and allow the FADEC laws* to adjust the fuel flow as needed. There's no need to drain the battery bringing the temperature down and then bringing it up again.

For older engines without FADECs, it may be best to do a venting run.

Note: You should always be focussed on T4 during a start and be prepared to abort if a hot start is indicated. Also, the above depends on a strong battery - the AS 350 is very sensitive to losing one or two volts.

Counting Engine Cycles

GAS GENERATOR EQUATION

$$N = K1 + (n \times K2)$$

where:

- K1 = Coefficient representing maximum N_G used
- K2 = Coefficient representing minimum N_G used
- n = partial cycles carried out between start and shutdown

A normal N_G cycle is one start and warmup, takeoff, and 30 sec ground idle cooldown. In that instance, your cycles would be determined by your maximum N_G, a K1 value.

A partial cycle is a power decrease followed by a significant increase without shutting down the engine. It may be defined as the number of hover events and landings. In short, the maximum N_G between starts equals K1, add the sum of all K2 events to obtain the cycles to log.

N$_G$ Measurement

B, B1, BA

This is a self-contained system that has a transmitter driven by the gas generator whose movements are reflected by an indicator in the cockpit. The general principle is shown below:

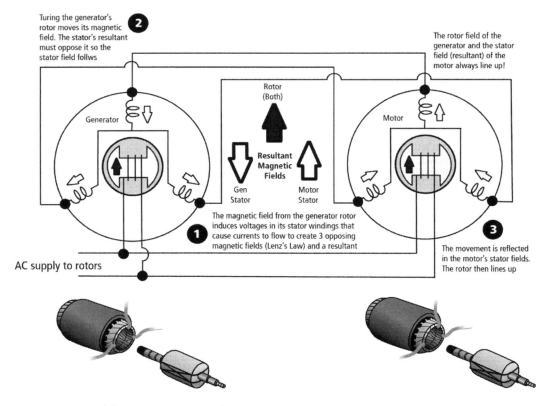

Turing the generator's rotor moves its magnetic field. The stator's resultant must oppose it so the stator field follws **2**

The rotor field of the generator and the stator field (resultant) of the motor always line up!

Rotor (Both)

Generator

Motor

Resultant Magnetic Fields

Gen Stator

Motor Stator

The magnetic field from the generator rotor induces voltages in its stator windings that cause currents to flow to create 3 opposing magnetic fields (Lenz's Law) and a resultant **1**

3

The movement is reflected in the motor's stator fields. The rotor then lines up

AC supply to rotors

The current put out by an AC generator on the engine has a frequency proportional to the N_G. It is fed to the receiver which is a synchronous motor that drives a magnet. The magnet induces a torque (with the use of eddy currents) on an aluminium disc that is attached to a pointer inside the RPM gauge. The torque, which is balanced by a spiral spring, is proportional to magnet RPM, and therefore N_G.

B2

Here, the current is generated by a 2-pole transmitter driven by the engine's accessory gearbox. The output is transformed by a converter inside the indicator to a voltage that is proportional to engine RPM and displayed as $\%N_G$ on the digital readout.

T4 Measurement

The temperature of the gases is measured at the free turbine inlet by chromel-alumel thermocouples that put out a voltage that is proportional to the temperature being measured. There are three thermocouples, at 120° to each other, in the exhaust gas duct. They are parallel mounted, so that the millivoltmeter reads the highest voltage, and the highest temperature.

© *Phil Croucher, 2011*

AS 355

The N model is easiest to start as it's almost completely automatic. You still have to monitor the EGT, though, as there is no auto limiting during the start sequence. Having said that, the Arrius is far more stable than the Allisons fitted to the F1 and F2.

The engines can be started with the ECLs (Engine Control Levers, i.e. throttles) at either **GROUND** or **FLY**, which is useful for fast starts.

 If you do start the engines at **FLY** you MUST ensure that the collective is locked down (a precaution to be taken with all AS 350/355s).

Occasionally, the FADEC on the N series will get a Logic Lock and not let you start an engine. Shut everything down, switch off the batteries for 10 seconds, then try again.

Note: The F series is started with the generators on line. Doing it the 206 way (generator off) only serves to confuse everything and the generators go offline a lot more.

Allison 250

This is a *reverse-flow free turbine*, designated the (Rolls Royce) Allison 250-C20F, which weighs 158 lbs (reverse flow means that the turbine and combustion sections are not in the traditional order). There may be a suffix to denote special characteristics - for example, the only difference between a B and a J engine is the way some of the gears are cut in the accessory gearbox, which makes the J slightly quieter. On the 355, the letter simply means the drive comes out through the front of the engine as opposed to the back. The PTGs will also be different.

Essentially, a six-stage axial flow, one-stage centrifugal compressor is bolted to the front side of an accessory gearbox, and 2 two-stage turbines plus a combustion chamber are bolted to the rear.

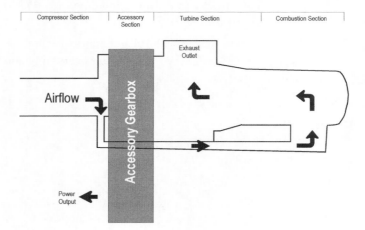

The first turbine (the gas producer, or N_1) drives the compressor itself, and the second (the power section, or N_2) drives the power output shaft (via a freewheel), which feeds into a reducing main rotor gearbox. Both turbines have two sets of blades, and the shafts are inside each other. 100% N_1 is actually 50,970 RPM, and 104% (the max) is 53,000.

Air is initially compressed to over 6 atmospheres (at 77 cubic metres a minute), then transferred to the combustion chamber at the rear, through two *air transfer tubes* that are visible on each side. The compressor casing is lined with plastic, and the rear face of the front diffuser is sprayed with aluminium which leaves tell-tale marks in the exhaust should the centrifugal compressor contact it. The front (No 1) bearing has a hollow front support which can use the anti-ice bleed from the compressor. There is a bleed valve at the fifth stage of compression, which is open during start, acceleration and low compressor pressure ratio operations, fully closing at 87% N_1. The idea is to unload the compressor and prevent blade stall and surge. The bleed valve should be wedged closed during compressor washing, and you should be able to see through it before you go flying.

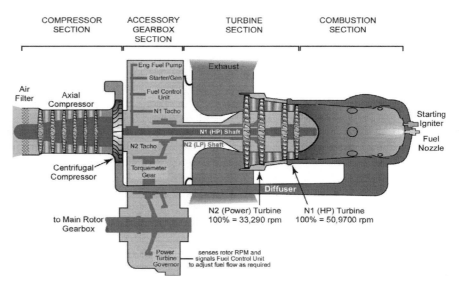

The air passing through the compressor is above the speed of sound at normal temperatures, but as the temperature is also very high, this velocity can be achieved with little trouble.

The combustion chamber is a single burner can at the rear of the engine with a single duplex burner and an igniter plug at the rear face. Inside, the air ducts are shaped so the flame does not come into contact with the casing, or any other part of the engine, but is contained within a cocoon of cooler air called a *toroidal vortex*, which is why the intake air is ducted along both sides of the engine, through 180° and up through the hot section in the direction of travel, for better control. In fact, 60-80% of the air sucked in the front is for cooling (roughly the equivalent of a large house every minute).

The fuel nozzle has two holes - the smaller primary one in the centre is used for the starting fuel, and the secondary, which surrounds it, opens when fuel pressure reaches 150 psi. The two together supply fuel for higher power settings. Fuel nozzles are highly polished and must be handled very carefully. In particular, they should never be brushed clean, as even a small scratch will affect the spray pattern, which will burn turbine wheels, etc.

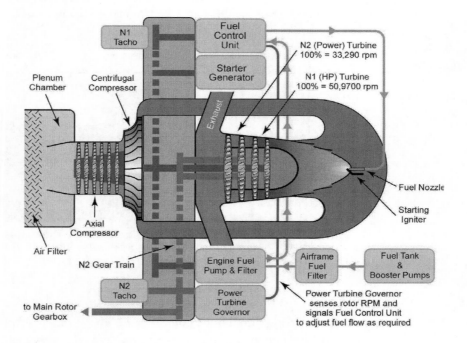

Each turbine drives a gear train in the accessory gear train. The gas producer also drives:

- the engine fuel pump
- N_1 tacho (and generators)
- oil pumps
- starter/generator
- centrifugal oil/air separator

The power turbine drives the N_2 tacho and generator, and incorporates the torquemeter (tacho generators are 3-phase AC generators connected to 3-phase synchronous motors in the gauges in the cockpit). After passing forward through the turbines, the hot air is exhausted upwards through twin exhaust ducts. All this means the engine can occupy much less space.

Four bayonet-type thermocouples sense the temperature between the turbines to feed the TOT gauge with averaged readings. If you get an abnormally high reading, a thermocouple sensor may have gone to ground. As the N_1 turbine (the mini) works hardest and is in the hottest airstream, its service life is only half that of the power turbine.

Lubrication (see *Oil*, below) uses a circulating dry sump with an external reservoir and heat exchanger. Various pressure and scavenge pumps in the engine are driven by the accessory gear box. Only the pressure and scavenge lines to the front and rear bearings are external.

Firewall

To comply with Category A airworthiness standards, the engines in the AS 355 are separated by a titanium firewall which is supposed to protect the engines from each other if one catches fire for up to 15 minutes.

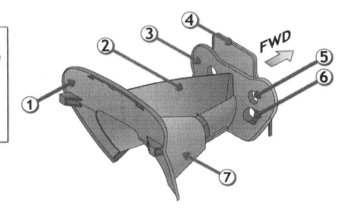

KEY:
1 - REAR FIREWALL (TITANIUM)
2 - REMOVABLE CENTER FIREWALL (TITANIUM)
3 - FORWARD FIREWALL (TITANIUM)
4 - MGB COWLING MOUNTS
5 - ENGINE AIR INTAKE DUCTS
6 - ENGINE MGB CONNECTING HOUSING PASSAGE
7 - TAIL ROTOR DRIVE SHAFT AND FAN ASSEMBLY TUNNEL (TITANIUM)

Overhead Panel

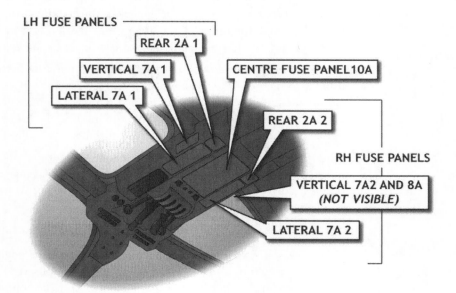

The throttles are on the overhead panel, with the engine start switch near the root. Interestingly, although the engine is the same one as in the Bell 206, the self sustaining speed is 60% in the AS 350, as opposed to 58%.

The red patches in the picture are the fuse panels.

Transmission & Rotors

The main rotor drive system transmits engine power to the main rotor shaft, at the same time reducing the output speed of the engine and changing its direction by around 90 degrees. The transmission cannot move vertically, so forces applied to it will be transmitted to the fuselage, or go back up to the head.

MAIN ROTOR GEARBOX

The main gearbox is in a fireproof bay, attached to the engine with a coupling shaft and a flexible input coupling. The shaft and coupling turn inside a flared coupling tube (see *Rigid Link*, overleaf).

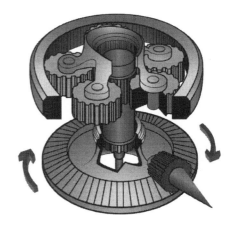

The insides are shown in the picture on the right. It is of a modular* design, including servo units, a rotor brake and a hydraulic pump drive.

Modular means that the gearbox has subassemblies that can be replaced without adjustment or special tooling, and without returning the gearbox to the factory. There are three modules - an epicyclic reduction gear with five planet gears, a bevel reduction gear in two casings, and a lubrication module on the lower casing.

There are two reduction stages, consisting of 1 bevel gear drive and 1 epicyclic gear train, transmitting engine power to the rotors, after a reduction of rotation speed. The casing also transmits main rotor reduction torque from the rotor shaft to the airframe.

The input pinion from the engine runs at 6000 RPM, and it has 17 teeth. As the ring gear has 61 teeth, the reduction ratio for the first stage is 3.69.

For the second stage, the sun gear has 30 teeth and the epicyclic 100 teeth. The reduction ratio is 4.33. The main rotor shaft runs at 386 RPM.

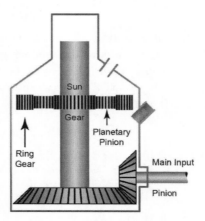

The 355's gearbox is of similar construction, except that a combining gearbox feeds the input from the two engines into the bevel gear drive.

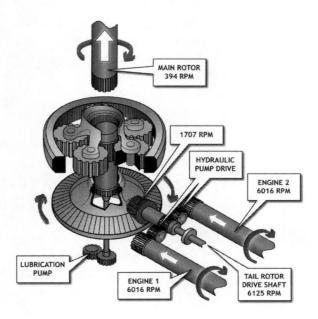

Suspension

The main rotor shaft produces periodic alternating vertical and horizontal loads. To stop them being transmitted to the airframe, the gearbox is pendulously suspended between 4 rigid bars that transfer the lift from the rotor to the structure.

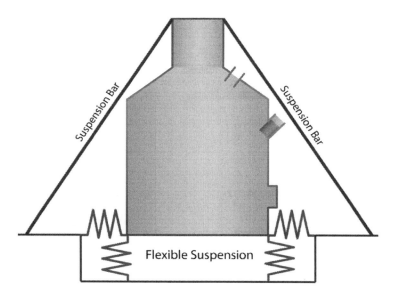

There are flexible bidirectional mountings at the bottom, consisting of cylindrical laminated pads made of thin rubber and light alloy (Duralumin) bonded together. One face is attached to the main gearbox, the other to the airframe.

Laminated pads are fail safe - any degradation takes place v e r y s l o w l y and can be easily spotted within maintenance time frames.

A damaged elastomeric will result in a medium frequency vibration of 3-6 per revolution.

The pads distort laterally to absorb vibrations. Main rotor reaction torque is transferred by compression.

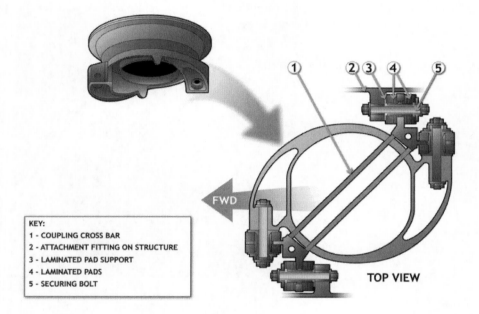

KEY:
1 - COUPLING CROSS BAR
2 - ATTACHMENT FITTING ON STRUCTURE
3 - LAMINATED PAD SUPPORT
4 - LAMINATED PADS
5 - SECURING BOLT

TOP VIEW

When the directions of the loads are reversed in autorotation, another laminated pad is compressed only when the torque direction is reversed. If one ruptures, the assembly is kept in place by a support.

The longitudinal and lateral pads do not have the same thickness.

Freewheel

The engine (inside the rear part of a coupling housing) transmits engine torque through a universal joint and an input pinion that includes a freewheel.

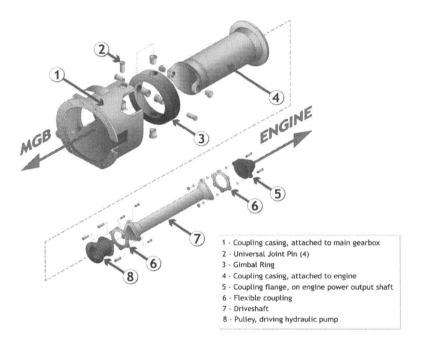

1 - Coupling casing, attached to main gearbox
2 - Universal Joint Pin (4)
3 - Gimbal Ring
4 - Coupling casing, attached to engine
5 - Coupling flange, on engine power output shaft
6 - Flexible coupling
7 - Driveshaft
8 - Pulley, driving hydraulic pump

RIGID LINK

The housing and barrel are there because the main rotor gearbox is mounted on a flexible suspension system which subjects it to low amplitude oscillations when in flight. The engine therefore has to move with it to prevent the drive shaft from being stressed too much.

The housing and barrel provide a rigid link between the engine and the main gearbox, to keep them aligned and oppose the engine overturning moment so that the coupling shaft only transmits engine torque.

To compensate for any misalignments between the engine and gearbox, the junction housing and barrel are connected with a gimbal ring which allows lateral and vertical movement.

FLEXIBLE LINK

There are flexible couplings between the drive shaft and the MGB input pinion. They distort to compensate for minor misalignments.

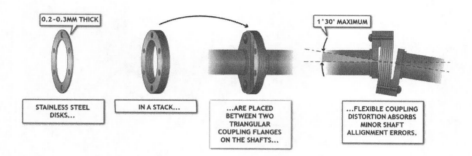

Because they transmit engine torque as well, they are subject to heavy operating loads in the shape of alternating fatigue stresses as the distortion is repeated every shaft rotation. They are designed to be fail safe.

FREEWHEEL

The freewheel only transmits motion from the engine to the rotors.

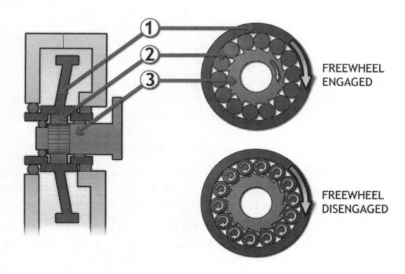

© *Phil Croucher, 2011*

Pre-mod TU 153, it is a sealed unit with its own oil supply (in a reservoir), so loss of engine oil pressure should not affect it. As there is little or no sprag contact in an autorotation, and the clutch should survive without oil, post-mod TU 153, the freewheel is lubricated by oil jet #18, with the pressure coming from engine oil pump.

Torquemeter

Turbine engines have a smooth and uniform torque output due to their continuous combustion. Torque is the measure of power being used, being a force applied at a distance by a turning point. It is measured between the engine and the reduction gearbox, and can be expressed in Newton metres, brake or shaft horsepower and inch or foot pounds. It may be shown on a torque gauge as a percentage.

$$Power = Torque \times RPM$$

The torquemeter needs to be on the output shaft because the drive shaft connecting the power turbine assembly must be as light as possible, so it only has a small margin of strength for excessive torque, or twisting, loads. Changes in the N_1 or TOT will be the only way of telling whether the engine is off specification, as the torque indication will always be the same.

AS 350

Engine torque is measured at the intermediate pinion of the engine reduction gear. As it has helical teeth, it produces a sideways thrust and reaction proportional to engine torque as the gears try to separate (because engine torque and the resistance of the rotor drive system oppose each other).

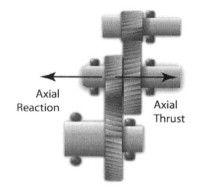

Axial Reaction

Axial Thrust

Oil from the engine lubricating pump flows into a torquemeter measuring chamber (through a restrictive nozzle) and out through a leakage port whose opening varies with the pinion position. As the piston moves to slow down the leakage as torque increases, the pressure increases inside the chamber, and *vice versa*. As the pressure inside the chamber is proportional to the engine torque, you can measure torque from a simple pressure measurement, hence the use of a Bourdon tube (3).

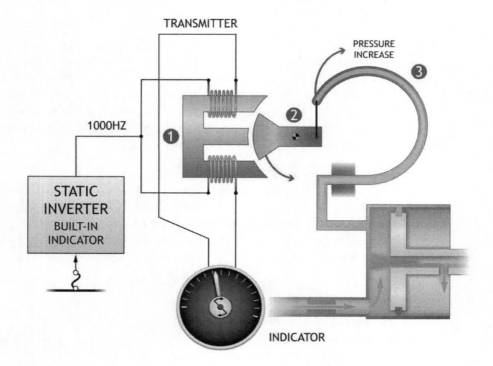

The above is an inductive system that uses moveable vane (2) inside the magnetic field generated by coils on mild iron armatures that are energised with AC at a frequency of 1000 Hz. As the Bourdon tube moves with the pressure, it moves the vane which changes the status of the magnetic field on the armatures - each pressure value corresponds to a given vane position and a value of reluctance for each coil, which is transmitted to the indicator.

AS 355

Similar principles apply to the Allison engines in the AS 355.

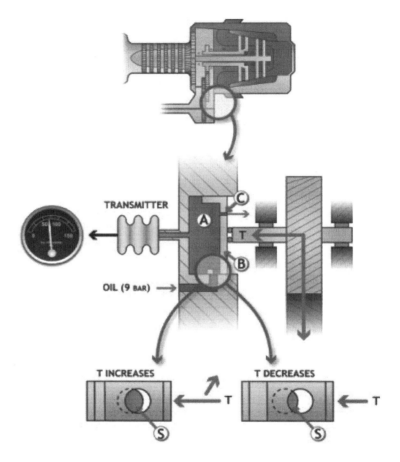

Engine oil flows into the measuring chamber (A), then out through a leakage port (C). The piston (B) is moved by the axial thrust (T), to change the size of the hole in the oil inlet (S) into the torquemeter chamber. As the cross section of the leakage port does not change, oil pressure varies according to the variations at S, in that, if torque increases, so does T, and the piston (B) moves inwards to make the hole at S bigger, and the pressure inside the chamber increases. The reverse if torque decreases.

If the helical gears move too much, they will no longer mesh correctly, so you need some method (in this case, oil pressure) to keep them in place. Engine oil is boosted to a high pressure (around 800 psi) and fed inside the cylinders which form the bearings around which the helical gears rotate. A small bleed hole in the wall of the cylinder is covered if the gear moves under load, which increases the oil pressure enough to move it back. If the load decreases, the existing oil pressure forces the shaft slightly out of the cylinder so the hole is uncovered.

This allows the balancing oil pressure to be reduced to move the gear back within the cylinder.

LUBRICATION

· ·

The gears and bearings of the main gearbox are lubricated with a pressurised oil system. The bottom of the casing is used as an oil tank.

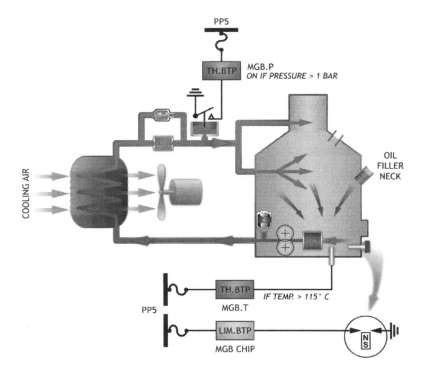

A gear-type pump pulls the oil from the bottom of the main gearbox and delivers it under pressure to a cooler. The cooled oil is filtered before it enters the main gearbox where it is sprayed onto gears and bearings through oil jets. Gravity is used to drain it down to the bottom of the case.

The relief valve opens during cold weather starting if the oil pressure gets up to 6.5 bar. The amount of oil passing through the cooler is therefore reduced and the temperature of the oil increases quicker.

The motor driven fan draws air through the cooler, usually in the hover. It is controlled automatically by the temperature of the engine oil.

The oil must be:

- Of sufficient quantity
- Clean
- Changed at regular intervals

Check the flight manual for approved oils.

Note: Mixing synthetic oil with mineral oil is not allowed.

On the 355, at the gearbox oil outlet, the temperature is around 120° so it is cooled in an external heat exchanger that removes the heat equivalent of 16 KW.

ROTOR HEAD

The Starflex **semi-rigid** main rotor head is made from resin glass fibre, laminated thrust bearings and self-lubricating bearings, all elastomeric (see right). It has no "proper" bearings, drag dampers or grease nipples.

Each arm is made of resin and glass cloth, which is moulded and cured in an oven.

The star has three arms that are flexible in a flapping sense, and rigid dragwise, meaning that they move up and down easily, but not horizontally.

The laminated spherical bearing is flexible in torsion, flapping and drag, but rigid in compression. All motions and loads pass through it.

The swashplate is operated by three mobile cylinder servo controls (two lateral, one fore-and-aft) whose piston rod is integral with the main gearbox. Control movements are transmitted to the starflex, which bends to control rotor pitch.

here is a vibration dampening device in the centre of the rotor head, which consists of a weight oscillating between three springs 120° apart.

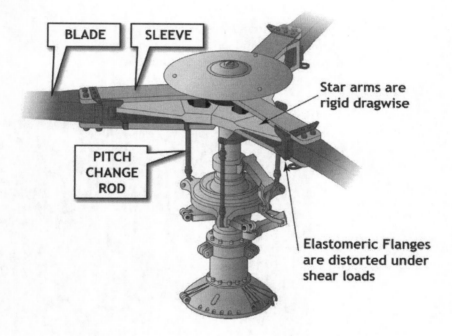

Tip: To help protect the starflex on sloping ground, once both skids are down, centralise the cyclic, as the machine will be going nowhere and any strain is reflected in the starflex. It doesn't give any immediate benefit, but will be reflected in maintenance costs.

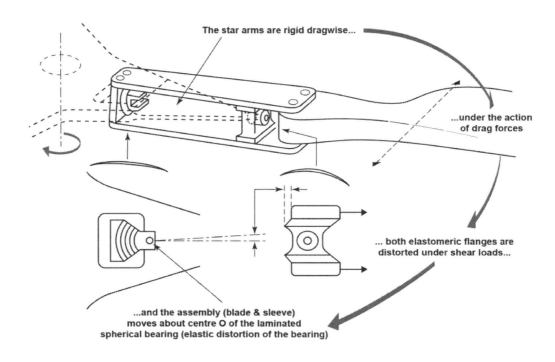

The star arms are rigid dragwise...

...under the action
of drag forces

... both elastomeric flanges are
distorted under shear loads...

...and the assembly (blade & sleeve)
moves about centre O of the laminated
spherical bearing (elastic distortion of the bearing)

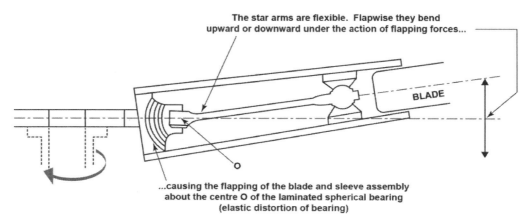

The star arms are flexible. Flapwise they bend
upward or downward under the action of flapping forces...

BLADE

...causing the flapping of the blade and sleeve assembly
about the centre O of the laminated spherical bearing
(elastic distortion of bearing)

Rotor Mast

The main rotor mast has removable sub assemblies. The mast casing is attached by four suspension bars that "carry" the aircraft.

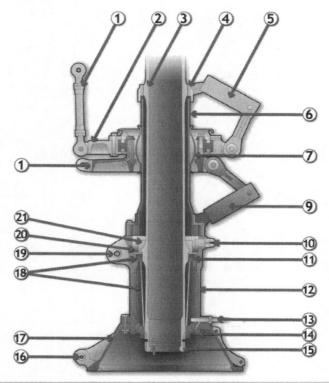

KEY:

1 - PITCH-CHANGE ROD	11 - ROLLER OR TAPER ROLLER BEARING
2 - ROTATING SWASHPLATE	12 - UPPER HOUSING (LIGHT ALLOY)
3 - ROTOR SHAFT (STEEL)	13 - OIL JET FOR BEARINGS 11 AND 14
4 - SCISSORS DRIVE ADAPTER	14 - 4-CONTACT OR TAPER ROLLER BEARING
5 - ROTATING SCISSORS	15 - SHAFT DRIVE SPLINES
6 - SWASHPLATE GUIDE	16 - SERVOCONTROL ATTACHMENT YOKE
7 - SPHERICAL BEARING (FORMED STEEL SHEET)	17 - CONICAL HOUSING (LIGHT ALLOW)
8 - SELF-LUBRICATING ADHESIVE TAPE	18 - BEARING SPACER AND SHIM
9 - NONROTATING SCISSORS	19 - SUSPENSION BAR ATTACHMENT FITTING
10 - TACHOMETER SENSOR	20 - LIP SEAL
	21 - SLOTTED WHEEL TO MEASURE ROTOR RPM
	22 - NONROTATING SWASHPLATE

The shaft is driven by the main gearbox, and the fixed star (swashplate) is moved by the flight controls at 3 points.

The fixed star is mounted on a ball joint that slides up and down on a guide during movement of the collective lever. The rotating star (on another bearing) follows the motions of the fixed star and transmits them to the blade horns by three pitch change rods.

Except for normal visual checks, no servicing is required on the rotor shaft.

ROTORS

The rotors, which are made of glass-resin laminate, go round clockwise when viewed from above. Pitch variation is achieved through distortion of elastomer items. The yellow blade is the master.

The spar of the blade consists of two glass rovings wound around blade attachment bushes, placed in a mould and hot cured. Afterwards, the core assembly is wrapped in 4 plies of glass yarn that cross alternately at 45°.

The resins used are sensitive to ultra-violet rays, so they are protected with polyurethane paint.

The blades are attached to the sleeves with two pins held in place by a locking (nappy) pin. Each blade has another safety pin to perform the same function for double safety. There is a bonding braid to ensure electrical continuity between the metal parts of the blade and the rotor head.

Rotor Speed

A horn sounds when speed drops below 360 RPM.

Rotor speed is detected with a phonic wheel and a magnetic probe.

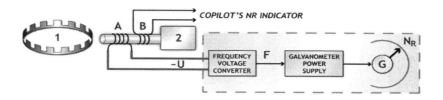

When a tooth passes in front of the sensor, the magnetic flux is maximum (it is minimum when a slot passes by). The pulses have a frequency equal to the number of variations per second. As the number of teeth stays the same, the signal frequency is proportional to rotor RPM.

A frequency-voltage converter transforms the signals into DC so that the tachometer receives a current proportional to rotor RPM. The signals are also sent to a frequency detector that operates the horn control circuit between 250 and 335 RPM. The horn also operates when hydraulic pressure gets below 30 bar.

Rotor Brake

The rotor brake (on the input to the main gearbox) is there to stop the rotors quickly after shutting down the engine(s), for safety and convenience. It also stops the rotors turning under the influence of wind when the machine is parked.

The kinetic energy is absorbed by the friction of linings on a disk that is driven by the tail rotor drive shaft. Because this creates heat that may damage the disk and pads, rotor brakes should not be applied above a certain RPM.

The maximum RPM speed for the rotor brake is 170 RPM in heavy winds (140 in light), with at least 5 minutes between actuations.

Note: The centrifugal force on the blades plays a major part in their stiffness. As they slow down, the brake force can cause excessive edgewise stresses as they are forced forward when the hub slows down rapidly. Thus, the blade is getting less stiff and the brake is getting proportionally stronger as the rotor energy decays rapidly with RPM.

When the lever is forward, the rotor brake is released. When applied, the lever causes a diaphragm spring to compress, which keeps the friction linings under constant load.

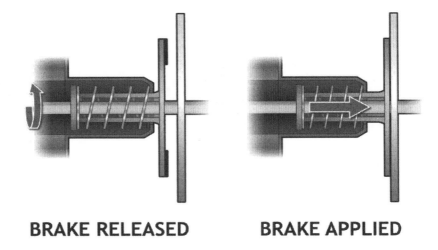

BRAKE RELEASED   **BRAKE APPLIED**

TAIL ROTOR

There is a two-piece drive shaft for the tail rotor - the second is supported by five ball bearing assemblies.

The tail rotor itself is two-bladed, and see-saw mounted on the tail rotor gearbox. Blade construction is similar to that of the main rotor blades.

The blade spar (a thin, flat rectangular blade) is made of fibreglass rovings, with no hinge and no lubrication. The pitch is changed by twisting the spar. The volume between the spar and the skin is filled with a foam-type substance (alkyd isocyanate).

It rotates anticlockwise as viewed from the right, so it is a pusher. Be aware that over-stuffing the rear baggage compartment can affect the controls as they are routed just above the compartment.

The extra bit of metal along the trailing edges of the blades must be checked for cracks regularly at each end, where they are riveted.

Chinese Weights

On any blade, centrifugal force emanates from all points, rather than just along its length:

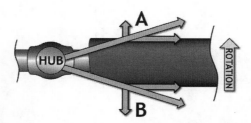

The outgoing vectors can resolve into two components - one parallel to the blade axis and one perpendicular which creates a moment around the feathering axis.

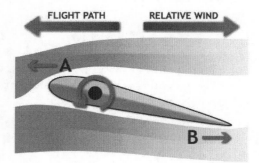

Because of the angles involved, the moment at the trailing edge of a blade (B) is longer than the one on the leading edge (A), and it not in line with the other in flight, so a couple is created that feathers the blade and makes it throw off pitch. This effect is called the *Zero Pitch Return Moment*. It is a particular problem with tail rotors.

On the 350/355 it is alleviated by a counterweight above the pitch change axis. The *Chinese weight* is perpendicular to the aerofoil to create a moment to counteract the zero pitch tendency.

Tail Rotor Gearbox

The tail rotor gearbox changes the direction of drive and reduces speed by a factor of about 3:1 (the tail rotor drive shaft runs at 6 000 RPM (6125 in the BA), which is reduced to 2043 (2085) for the tail rotor). It is splash-lubricated with 0.8 gals of oil, which is topped up through a filler hole on the top of the gearbox housing.

In the lower part of the gearbox housing is a metal chip warning sensor, which has two magnetic poles to attract any metal chips in the oil. If they gather between the poles there will be a connection, the warning system is activated and a lamp in the cockpit comes on. The hole in the gearbox housing for the sensor also acts as a drain hole for the gearbox oil.

There is no system for measuring and indicating the oil level or temperature during flight. Instead, the level is checked before flight with a sight glass that is visible through a hole in the left side of the gearbox cover. Markings on the sight glass show the lowest and highest oil levels for flight.

Note; The oil level in the sight glass is affected by how the helicopter is standing when parked. If the oil has drained out (or has not been replaced during an inspection), the oil visible in the sight glass is residual oil that is stuck, due to capillary action, on the inside of the glass. On a preflight inspection, depending on the viewing angle, it could look as if the oil is a little low, but enough for flight.

Picture: AS 350 somewhere way up North (courtesy, Great Slave Helicopters)

SYSTEMS

This section covers most of the aircraft systems.

HYDRAULICS

The hydraulic system is there to reduce your workload by making the controls lighter in normal flight, as the forces involved would be severe without them. In fact, at high speeds, they are considered to be excessive, so machines which have only one hydraulic system (the B4 and 355 have two) have a "safety unit" on each servo which consists of an accumulator, a non-return valve and a solenoid valve, designed to give you enough time to get the speed back to where the machine is controllable, between 40-60 kts.

Note: The AS 350 is a great ship to fly, but it is most important that you thoroughly understand the operation of the hydraulic system, as it is non-standard in many ways, as described below.

Note: When the hydraulics fail, the tail rotor pitch will take up a neutral setting because there is a twist in the spar of the tail rotor which makes it do so. In the hover, this will make the nose turn to the left, which could be mistaken for a tail rotor failure*, as the controls are still boosted by the accumulators, if only for a short while.

In this case, a little right pedal is needed (plus some forward and left cyclic in the cruise) as aerodynamic effects on the main rotor will push the cyclic aft and to the right.

*The aft and right cyclic movement will cause the nose to pitch upwards and the vertical stabiliser to reduce its effectiveness as you slow down. This will cause the nose to go to the left.

The AS 350's hydraulic system is unique in several ways:

- The hydraulic pressure is relatively low at 40 bar (around 580 psi). The S-76, in contrast, uses 3,000 psi, which allows more energy to be transmitted with smaller piston areas, so it saves weight. In fact, 3,000 psi is now considered to be out of date! The S-92 uses 4,000 psi.

- The variable delivery hydraulic pump is belt-driven (but some variations, particularly military ones, use gears).

- The hydraulic jacks are attached directly to the transmission (as opposed to the airframe), so the swashplate is supported by them.

- Each servo has an accumulator, which makes the transition from hydraulics on to hydraulics off less abrupt.

- It only has a warning light (as opposed to a caution light) to warn of loss of hydraulic pressure, but it also uses......

- a warning horn, which is shared with the low rotor RPM warning. Either failure will make it sound. Both failures produce the same tone.

- There is a hydraulics test system (through a **HYD TEST** pushbutton on the centre console) separate from the hydraulic cutoff system.

- There is (now) a Flight Manual Supplement (since 2005) discussing hydraulics off training in great detail, *from the cruise only*, which implies that simulated hydraulics failure in any other situation is not recommended. As well, that there is little room for error, otherwise the supplement would not have been issued 25 years after the type first entered service. It was added after a particular accident.

- The collective lever has to be locked down during hydraulic checks, meaning that it is specifically excluded from them. Other helicopters require all their controls to be moved, to ensure that there is no jamming when hydraulic assistance is not available. If the collective is not locked down (and at least one of the servo accumulators is exhausted), when the cutoff switch is selected OFF, it can raise itself and allow the helicopter to become airborne (without hydraulics).

It is not clear what causes the collective to rise. As no servo has any hydraulic pressure and there is initially no collective pitch applied to the main rotor blades, it may be that the elastomeric bearings in the main rotor head are seeking a minimum force position, which roughly corresponds to the setting for 40-60 knots of airspeed. This up force can mostly be overcome when there are no hydraulics, although there have been at least two occasions when this has not been the case.

- The hydraulic system cannot overcome the forces imposed on the flight control system created by aggressive manoeuvres (within the flight envelope!) without changing the feel of the controls and the forces required to fly the helicopter. This servo transparency (jackstall) is unique to Eurocopter helicopters and is found on the AS-350 family, the SA-365 early 4 bladed series, and the SA-341 Gazelle.

- It is the only light helicopter with a Main Servo-Control Slide-Valve Seizure emergency procedure in the flight manual that is different than the normal loss of hydraulic pressure procedure, if only because there are no symptoms listed (at least in the B2 flight manual). There are no warning lights, caution lights, audio or vibratory signals, so it would be hard to recognize the problem if it happens.

- There is no hydraulic system pressure gauge in the cockpit, nor is there a static pressure monitoring device for the accumulators.

Accumulators

One of the principles of the AS 350's certification (by Transport Canada, at least) was the provision of a flight control system that, if the main hydraulic system failed, allowed you to continue to manipulate the flight controls with reasonable feedback forces. The safety unit (including the accumulator) was added for that purpose, to establish a safety speed. Thus, the accumulators are an intrinsic part of the hydraulic system and crucial to its function, hence the pre-flight test described later.

An accumulator is a sturdy container attached to each hydraulic jack (servo) as part of the safety unit.

Part of its job is to store energy in the form of hydraulic fluid under pressure that can be used for a short time if the main system fails or needs help at peak times - that is, in a failure, you can still move the controls for a few seconds, at least enough to bring the speed back to where the forces are controllable. The stored pressure also allows an initial impetus to be given when a selection is made (that is, it reduces lag in the system). You can also think of an accumulator as a shock absorber, since a valve opening in a pressurised system can make quite an impact on the hydraulic lines. Yet another function is to use the stored pressure to reduce the number of times the hydraulic pump has to switch on and off when there is low demand, which saves wear and tear. As the output from an accumulator can be more (temporarily) than that from the system anyway, you can then save weight and expense by using pumps of lesser capacity, and size.

Inside an accumulator, a piston or a diaphragm separates hydraulic fluid under normal system pressure from an inert gas (nitrogen at 15 bar in the case of the AS 350) which is also under pressure, having been charged up on the ground. An inert gas is used because oxygen and oil can become explosive if you combine them under high pressure.

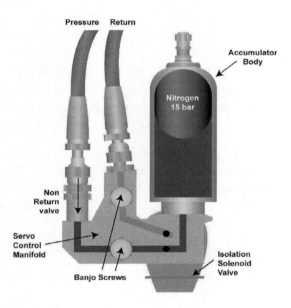

As soon as the system pressure drops, the nitrogen expands against the bladder to force the fluid out on the other side, which keeps the system pressurised for a short while.

Depending on how much and how harshly you use the controls, the accumulators will usually bleed off their stored pressure inside about 20-30 seconds (the pitch servo may deplete first due to an initial nose-down tendency), which is time enough to bring the speed back and reduce the control forces, but you can expect the loads to increase again when you slow down for short finals. For this reason, you should always run-on with about 10 kts over the disc - *do not try to hover.*

It is not a good practice to try and land on accumulator pressure alone - for one thing, accumulators will not discharge at the same rate and, for another, they only work if you have fluid in the system, and you have no way of knowing what you have until you land - the reason for a run-on landing on any machine. You might easily find yourself in the hover with only fore and aft control.

Once you are at a manageable speed, you must operate the hydraulic cutoff switch (on the collective) to activate the solenoids that will ensure that the accumulators are completely discharged *simultaneously*, so you don't get an asymmetric condition. You are then operating the controls manually.

Note: An uncommanded cyclic movement is possible when one lateral accumulator has less of a charge than the other. This is prevented in flight by following the Flight Manual procedure - i.e. when the hydraulics fail, slow down promptly to the specified speed and activate the hydraulic cutoff on the collective. If your machine has modified SAMM servos, an uncommanded input is also possible when pressurising the system (on start, or during the preflight check), where the centring pins can retract at different times - Eurocopter suggest using WD 40 but, for ultimate safety, do not repressurise the system in flight - once in manual control, stay there!

Components

On the average AS 350 (not the B4), the system comprises (see overleaf):

- a hydraulic reservoir (1) back of the main gearbox on the right, made of light aluminium alloy. It holds 2.1 litres of hydraulic fluid and feeds the pump by gravity (the total system volume is 3 litres).

- a belt-driven gear-type pump (2) on the right hand side of the main gearbox compartment, just behind the transmission. The belt is driven by the engine-main gearbox shaft. There are two types of belt, either green Filon or a black V Polychloroprene Polybutadiene, which are not interchangeable. Black ones last longer.

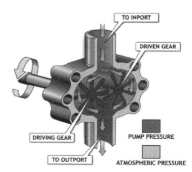

The pump can produce a flow rate of 6 litres per minute, even down to 170 N_R, although it can always produce something whenever the main rotors are turning. However, in cold weather (under - 25°C) the hydraulic fluid's viscosity increases and the belt can start to slip as it tries to cope. Friction eventually causes the belt to deform and stop turning the pump. It may even slip off the drive wheel.

- A hydraulic distribution block (3), on the right side of the main gearbox that receives pressurised fluid from the pump through the filter. The distribution block houses the filter clogging indicator, pressure relief valve (12), hydraulic pressure switch (10) and the hydraulic test solenoid (11). The filter has no bypass capability, so if it gets clogged, the fluid will not reach the servos. An indicator button will extend from the bottom of the filter housing when there is a 2.7 bar pressure differential across the filter, indicating potential clogging. The pressure relief valve (12) opens at around 40 bar to allow fluid to get back to the reservoir if system pressure gets too high. The low pressure switch (10) activates when the pressure drops below around 32 bar, illuminating the red **HYD** warning light on the warning panel and producing a continuous tone from the horn.

- Four identical* servos (4). There are three main ones: a forward one for pitch control, and left and right ones for roll. The fourth is used on the tail rotor and is in the forward end of the tail boom just under the tail rotor drive shaft - the B1 & B2 also have a yaw load compensator which assists with pedal inputs after a hydraulic failure, as the pedals would be very hard to manage otherwise.

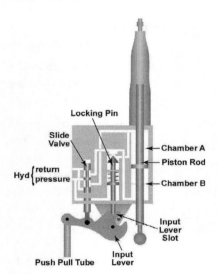

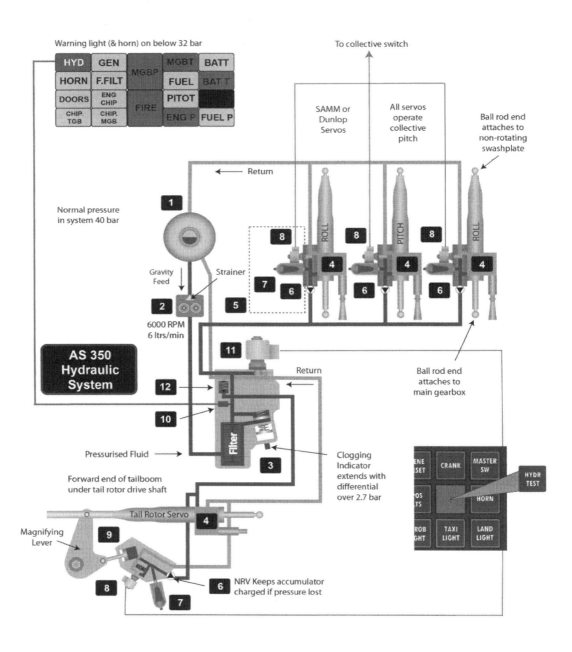

Warning light (& horn) on below 32 bar

To collective switch

Normal pressure in system 40 bar

SAMM or Dunlop Servos

All servos operate collective pitch

Ball rod end attaches to non-rotating swashplate

Return

Gravity Feed

Strainer

6000 RPM 6 ltrs/min

AS 350 Hydraulic System

Return

Ball rod end attaches to main gearbox

Pressurised Fluid

Clogging Indicator extends with differential over 2.7 bar

Forward end of tailboom under tail rotor drive shaft

Tail Rotor Servo

Magnifying Lever

NRV Keeps accumulator charged if pressure lost

*There are two manufacturers - Dunlop and SAMM. Although their products are functionally identical, Dunlops allow better control fore and aft if the hydraulics fail, and leak a lot less. As well, Dunlops only have a locking pin on the pitch servo.

Each main rotor servo includes a servo control manifold (5), which contains a non-return valve (6), an accumulator (7) and an isolation solenoid valve (8) that allows pressurised fluid to bypass the servo and return to the reservoir once the switch on the collective is operated. The non-return (or one-way check) valve (6) traps any pressure created by the accumulator in the lines after a pressure failure.

Hydraulic fluid enters the servo through the one way check valve. The fluid is routed to the accumulator, then to the inlet pressure port of the servo housing through a banjo screw, which is hollow, to allow the servo control manifold to be attached to the servo while hydraulic fluid flows. The slide valve routes the fluid to the relevant chamber, according to the desired direction of movement, while allowing fluid from the other chamber to be expelled through the banjo screw.

Unlike the main servos, the tail rotor system is designed to provide an almost unlimited supply of reserve pressure. If the pressure within it exceeds 55 bar, the check valve opens the pressure line to allow a partial hydraulic flow as the servo piston returns to the extend position. This prevents hydraulic locking and causes the stored pressure to be reduced.

• Various lights, button, switches and horns in the cockpit.

The hydraulic oil lines run through the inside of the main gearbox, so the fluid is kept warm. However, if you are not moving the controls, meaning that no oil is circulating, when sitting on the ground for a while, the oil in the servos may cool enough to cause any water contamination to freeze.

If the hydraulics fail, a **CUTOFF** switch on the collective is used to depressurize the accumulators by simultaneously opening the three main rotor dump valves (i.e. solenoids on the servos), to allow hydraulic fluid back to the reservoir and a smooth transition to manual control.

A toggle switch labelled **HYD TEST** (previously **ACCU TEST**), on the centre console tests the main- and tail rotor servo accumulators by opening test and tail-rotor servo solenoid valves, causing hydraulic pressure to drop and the warning light and horn to come on. In other words, it simulates a failure of the hydraulic pump and is a way of testing for the asymmetric problem - it is actually the accumulator test. If you push this button with there is no hydraulic pressure, you will purge the accumulator in the yaw compensator, standard procedure after shutdown.

Note: You should never have both switches off at the same time. NEVER touch the console **HYD TEST** button in flight when a real hydraulic failure is suspected, as it would render the tail rotor unusable (B2 & B3). In fact, you will be outside the certification limits. You will certainly need heavy pedal pressure and the yaw may well be uncontrollable to the left when you reduce airspeed (not to mention a heavy cyclic). The B3 has bigger tabs on the tail rotor blade than the B2, so this condition will be exacerbated, which is possibly why they replaced the yaw compensator on the B3e with additional boss weights on the tail rotor blades to help with the right pedal if the hydraulics fail. At least you won't hit the wrong switch.

If you have a hydraulic pump failure (in a machine with the yaw compensator) and engage the HYD TEST button, you will not get the compensator back as you have depressurised it. As you have no pump, it cannot be repressurised!

The only time you should touch **HYD TEST** in flight is when you suspect a tail rotor control problem and you need to have them somewhere near neutral (your pedals might be stuck). You might not get control back, but you do at least have a chance to run it on.

Examiners: Just hit the warning light button (and the horn) and call out the emergency. The student should slow down to 65kts and switch off the **HYD** switch on the collective, then slow down a bit more to about 55-60. If correctly tested at startup (see overleaf), the accumulators should provide enough pressure and time to slow to 60 kts, so this should be transparent, whether the **HYD TEST** button is pressed or not. As well, this avoids possible confusion in a real emergency, where the **HYD TEST** button may be used out of habit. Thus, if the hydraulics have a problem while you are practicing failures, the tail rotor stays controllable and a non-hydraulic landing should be no problemo. If you had the **HYD TEST** switch pressed or locked, you would add a tail rotor control failure to the emergency!

Note: Some amendments to various flight manuals correctly state that you should operate the collective switch, but not that you should reset it!

Hydraulic System Checks

The flight manual requires two hydraulic system tests after every start.

They were originally done on the ground at normal flying rotor speed (at least 375 RRPM) so that hydraulic operating pressure and volume are consistent with normal flight. However, full operating pressure is actually achieved at around 50% RRPM, and the flight manuals on the BB, D, B1, B2 and B3 have been revised to do the checks at ground idle, so at least the machine won't now get airborne by itself if the collective lock is disengaged.

Note: The tests also require that the collective be locked down. The spring steel locking plate should engage into a machined groove in a button at the end of the collective, pushing down on which releases it. However, on older ships, the plate can catch on the shoulder to the rear, outside the machined groove.

This condition takes less force to release the plate and is not easily detected. It is easy to bump the plate (and the collective) free by accident.

THE ACCUMULATOR TEST

This allows you to check that the accumulators are fully pressurised and would actually provide assistance if the system fails (for at least two flight control movements), plus the **HYD** warning light and horn (you cannot check the pressure of an accumulator in a pre-flight inspection).

Note: The accumulators are the sole approved mechanical devices providing any guarantee of reasonable feedback forces if the hydraulics fail. **You may not fly with an unserviceable accumulator.** This test is the last opportunity of making sure that they work, but there have been many undetected undercharged accumulators, ranging between 35 - 175 psi, where 218 psi would have been expected, so there is a question as to its effectiveness.

- Check that the collective is securely locked down by the locking strip and release the cyclic friction.

- Cut off the hydraulic pressure with **HYD TEST**. The solenoid valves on the distribution block and yaw load compensator should open.

- The pressurised fluids will return to the reservoir, so there will be no more hydraulic fluid flowing to the main and tail rotor servos, and they will be powered only by their accumulators (the tail rotor servo on the BA will no longer be pressurised). The decreasing pressure will cause the pressure switch to activate the **HYD** light and the horn, which you can deactivate to make things quiet again.

- Move the cyclic fore and aft 2-3 times for about 4 inches*, to check the pitch servo. Then move it left and right the same way for the roll servos. If you feel any control feedback, the accumulators need checking, as they are not doing their job.

- Move the tail rotor pedals left and right to check that the solenoid valve on the compensator body has dumped the pressure - the pedals should become stiff.

- Disengage the **HYD TEST** push button, re-engage the **HORN** button, and confirm that the **HYD** light has gone out.

*It is not clear what constitutes failing the test in terms of the number of movements of the cyclic before the accumulators deplete, as there is no flight manual requirement to exhaust them.

From AS 350BA, B-2 Ref 0 07-98:

> *"During each of the two hydraulics tests, the cyclic should not be driven laterally or longitudinally across the cabin during the cut off of hydraulics or during the restoration of hydraulics. If this occurs, it can be an indication that one of the accumulators is not fully charged or that a servo is defective."*

As for the last sentence, how can you tell if the problem is an accumulator that is not charged or a defective servo? A Telex issued on 9 Dec 2003 states:

> *"As the accumulators are depressurized, when restoring the hydraulic power system, it will take some time until the pressure rises to the nominal operating level. Normally this period covers 2 to 3 seconds, but is reduced to 1 second if at least one of the accumulators is incorrectly pressurized. (underlining in original). This pressure replenishing time for the hydraulic power system is assessed according to the duration of the horn operation over this period, as the horn will stop when the nominal operating pressure is reached again.*
>
> *Thus the accumulators are checked for correct nitrogen pressurization before the hydraulic assistance is used up when testing the accumulators."*

This information does not appear in any flight manual or training material. In fact, the only training material on the AS 350 hydraulics system that covers this only states that you should listen for the horn to sound for 2-3 seconds. There is no indication that a shorter time indicates failing the test.

HYDRAULIC ISOLATION CHECK

This check tests the proper operation of the isolation solenoid valves on the main rotor servos, plus the one on the yaw load compensator, to ensure that the system can be disabled after a hydraulic failure or a slide valve seizure, which could cause a hardover. It also checks the accumulator recovery time.

- Check that the collective is securely locked down by the locking strip.

- Place the switch on the collective in the cut-off position, to open the isolation solenoid valves and connect the inlets and outlets of the servo control manifolds. Now, pressure cannot build up as the fluid is bypassing the pressure ports on the main servos to the reservoir.

- The pressure switch on the distribution block senses this and illuminates the **HYD** light (as activating the isolation switch or push button disables the horn relay, so you can still get a low RRPM warning, the horn does not sound).

- The cyclic and pedals* will almost immediately get stiff. The cyclic should be slightly displaced fore and aft and left and right to ensure proper responses.

  *With the loss of pressure, the tail rotor servo will no longer be receiving pressurized fluid. Displace the pedals left and right to check that the yaw load compensator (if there is one) has held its charge by confirming that the pedals are partially boosted.

- Return the isolation switch to its normal position to close the solenoids. Pressure will build up again, especially in the accumulators. The **HYD** light should take about 3-4 seconds to go out. If it takes any more than that, the accumulators are undercharged, which allows more hydraulic fluid in - this takes time. Any less (no faster than one second), they are overcharged, meaning that less hydraulic fluid can fit in and the accumulators will fill to capacity faster. An interval of one second or less means that at least one of the accumulators is defective.

© *Phil Croucher, 2011*

Problems

LOSS OF PRESSURE

Loss of pressure can result from:

- Hydraulic pump or belt failure

- Clogged filter

- Hydraulic line break

> *"If you lose the hydraulic assist in the flight controls, they become direct-link connections. Because of the dynamic forces on the rotating components, it's hard to handle with any finesse in a hover."*

Jim di Giovanna, former commander of the Los Angeles County Sheriff Dept.'s Aero Bureau, which flies 12 AS 350 B2s.

> *"The helicopter can be controlled without hydraulic servo actuators but the pilot has to exert considerable muscular effort, which is difficult to gauge accurately, and, in some cases of extended flight, may exceed the physical strength or endurance of an individual pilot."*

Transport Canada accident report, C-GBHH 2006

> *"The helicopter can be maneuvered without hydraulic assists, but this requires the pilot to apply non-negligible forces that are difficult to gauge."*

Eurocopter Training Manual

The warnings—a gong or horn, depending on the model, and a light on the annunciator panel—are triggered when pressure in the hydraulic system falls below 30 bar. If you get them in the cruise, reduce airspeed to 40-60 kt. The collective lever will adopt about the same position that it seeks during the hydraulic test procedures on the ground, so the collective force is zero when the spherical stops in the rotor head are neutral (+7° pitch) which, in forward flight, means between 40-60 kts. At this speed, no force is needed to keep the collective in its position. It is needed, however, to go faster or slower, up to 25-30 lbs to get up to 120 kts and from a hover, up to 25-30 lbs down force to get it down to flat pitch. In other words, for any pitch position above or below +7°, the force required increases with more or less pitch. So, letting go of the collective in a hover will not make the helicopter hit the ground. In fact, it will move up to the +7° pitch position*, and you must push the collective down to land.

*This tendency is why it must be locked down when testing the hydraulics.

The only pressure left in the system is from the accumulators on the pitch and roll servos. Once you're in the airspeed range, hit the Isolate switch on the collective to drain the accumulators all at the same time, avoiding an asymmetric condition

Once pressure is lost, the pressure switch (12) on the distribution block will activate the **HYD** light and the horn. The accumulators should provide enough fluid under pressure to allow the controls to be normally boosted for 20-30 seconds, depending on how much and how harshly the controls are moved. Smooth and limited control inputs should allow you to land from an IGE hover or to otherwise bring the speed back to 40-60 knots.

The yaw pedals on the B and BA will become stiff, and those on the B1 and B2 will feel partially boosted because of the yaw load compensator.

The actions in flight are:

- Calmly reduce collective and adjust airspeed to between 40-60 knots in level flight. The rotor blades have a positive pitch setting, so the collective will sit in more or less this position anyway. The cyclic, however, will want to move aft and to the right!

- Cut off hydraulic pressure with the collective switch, which should* turn the horn off and dump the pressure in the accumulators at the same time, to prevent an asymmetric condition. Control loads will be felt when collective pitch is increased, and on forward and left-hand cyclic movement. You may increase speed at this point, but control feedback will also increase.

  *A Complementary Flight Manual was published several years after the introduction of the AS 350B series in which Section 4.3 states:

  Failures will characterized by the following indications, some or all of which may be present, thus modifying the conventional failure cues:

  - *...Flight control force feedback on one or all controls*

  - *Flight control forces may vary differently with airspeed than they normally do (control forces may increase with decreasing airspeed, or be almost constant with varying airspeed)*

- *Lateral cyclic forces may be high to the LEFT, requiring the pilot to pull the cyclic RIGHT to maintain attitude.*

- *Flight control force feedback forces may be felt immediately upon component failure. There may be little or no delay between first indication and force-feedback.*

- *The hydraulic cut-off switch may not be effective in opening all the electro-valves and dumping all the pressure in the accumulators*

Note that the last point mentions that the hydraulic cut-off switch may not actually shut off the pressure!

The complementary flight manual (04-09) further states:

> *If the hydraulic cutoff switch is ineffective, the control forces should become normal (for hydraulics off) after all the accumulators have depleted.*

That's all well and good, but if the accumulators do not deplete equally (that event is unlikely because you will likely use more lateral than longitudinal control movements), you will be left with uneven control forces, which could be a problem if you are in a turn the wrong way when the hydraulics fail and you attempt to roll out and decelerate by simultaneously applying low control forces in pitch and high control forces in roll.

- The flight manual recommends that you land as soon as possible, so extended flight is not recommended, but you should still make a shallow approach over a clear landing area (runway? field?) and land with slight forward speed. Be ready for the cyclic wanting to travel aft and to the right, and the additional right pedal as collective pitch is increased, otherwise the machine will pitch up and rotate to the left.

- After landing, lower the collective and lock it down while guarding the cyclic, which will have become stiff after you operate the **CUTOFF** switch on the collective. Shut down the engine.

If you are in ground effect, you should naturally control any tendency for the helicopter to spin - without a yaw load compensator, this might be quite hard! If out of ground effect, you will need to get to the 40-60 knot speed range, but otherwise the operations are the same.

SLIDE VALVE SEIZURE

The servo input lever is moved in the relevant direction by the flying controls, which move the slide valve in the servo control manifold.

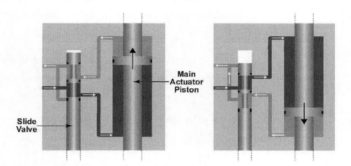

This routes the hydraulic fluid to the relevant side of the hydraulic piston to make it move in the desired direction.

If the slide valve seizes in any position besides hydraulic zero, fluid will continue to flow, and the cyclic (or pedals, if the tail rotor servo is affected) will move without your input. If the fluid pressure is not shut off, the helicopter may get into an unrecoverable attitude so, if the cyclic moves by itself, you should engage the isolation solenoid switch on the collective. The red **HYD** light will illuminate and the flight controls will immediately get stiff. If in the hover, you should land without delay.

Adjust the speed as quickly as possible and as best you can to the proper speed range.

The emergency procedure is:

- Actuate the (hydraulic) **CUTOFF** switch on the collective. Load feedback will be felt immediately, which may be heavy at high speed:

  - Collective: 20 kg pitch increase load

  - Cyclic: 7-4 kg left-hand cyclic load

  - Cyclic: 2-4 kg forward cyclic load

  - Pedals: Hardly any load in cruising flight

Reduce speed to 60 kts and proceed as for illumination of the **HYD** light.

Note the requirement to shut off the hydraulics first (or, rather, lower the collective later*), which is significantly different from the "normal" Loss of Hydraulic Pressure Emergency, where you first (calmly) obtain 40-60 knots, lower the collective (before the accumulators become fully discharged) and *then* shut off the hydraulics. Attending to the speed is the *last* step in the Main Servo-Control Slide-Valve Seizure procedure, so this is more serious than mere loss of hydraulics (if this emergency is the problem described in *Lettre-Service 1064067-91 30 Oct 91* (see below for extract), failure to turn off the hydraulics will lead to loss of control:

> *During a recent investigation, wear was found in the lateral servocontrol distributor valve drive. This wear leads to dissymmetry between the actuator extraction and retraction speeds. In flight, this phenomenon results in:*
>
> • *Resistance to rapid displacement of the stick in the direction of the incriminated servocontrol on the lateral axis.*
>
> • *Displacement on the roll axis in the opposite direction to the faulty lateral servocontrol during a rapid maneouvre on the collective axis.*
>
> *The emergency procedure in the event of a seizure of a distributor valve, which is described in the Flight Manuals, makes it possible to pass into a control mode without hydraulic assistance and thus cancels the effects of the problem.*

*As a single servo-control has seized in position, lowering the collective would make it act as a pivot point for the other two actuators. Normally, lowering the collective should result in an even movement of the swashplate.

Note: There have been reports of uncommanded cyclic movement when the hydraulics are already off, one to this author's knowledge during the preflight hydraulic check, *after* the accumulators were depleted. In fact, it was on 12 May 2003, on a B2 in Alberta. During this check and after the accumulators were depleted, the cyclic control moved uncommanded to an extreme left position. Considerable force was required to try to move it back. The uncommanded movement was repeatable, and is possible when one lateral accumulator is depleted and the other charged. However, uncommanded input is supposed to be prevented in flight when you slow down promptly to the specified speed and activate the hydraulic cut-off, where any unbalanced force from asymmetrical residual accumulator pressure is avoided. If the hydraulic cut-off is not activated, the sustained asymmetrical pressure may occur if the accumulator depletes at a different rate until the residual pressure is depleted through normal movement of the flight controls.

To check for this, (usually to the left), do a full hydraulics on check, then run the accumulators dry with the test switch, making sure that all is normal (for hydraulics off). Hit the switch again to recharge the accumulators, do a movement check, use the dump switch on the collective and recheck the movement. *Do not dump the hydraulics with the collective switch after running the accumulators dry before recharging them* - the collective switch may not be working and you won't even know (see overleaf). Obviously, land as soon as possible if you get a problem, and do the above check before *every flight*.

Note: There are no symptoms listed for this emergency (at least not in the B2 flight manual). There are no warning lights, caution lights, audio or vibratory signals, so it is unlikely that you would recognize the problem, so it is ultimately difficult to train for.

SERVO TRANSPARENCY (JACKSTALL)

This is a condition where the servos may stall under certain operating conditions and leave you with stiff or frozen cyclic and collective controls.

The phrase is a direct translation from the French, in which the jack appears to be no longer there.

Essentially, the stall on the retreating blade causes the blade to change its pitching moment sharply downward, which makes it try to dive. The strong downward force is fought by the pitch change links, swashplate and servos, and the loads on the main rotor head become too much for the system to cope with - the smaller blades on the AS 350B are particularly prone to it.

The conditions under which servo transparency occurs are supposed to be extreme, but have also been relatively benign, as when gently flying round a fire at 4,000 feet ASL on a warm day in a B model weighing 4000 lbs. In another example, the machine was descending from a mountain top at 110 kts with the collective fully down and well below gross weight. Windshear took the speed up to 155 kts and it snapped 90° to the right when the cyclic froze solid and both arms could not bring it back.

Some pilots in the Grand Canyon have experienced the phenomenon just on breezy days when the relative airflow is changing constantly.

© *Phil Croucher, 2011*

The hydraulics operate at lowish pressure, and when the forces down from the rotors equal the force the servos can send up, you will feel cyclic feedback, meaning that you have reached the G limit, although the controls should still work, with a little effort. This condition can be demonstrated by initiating a steep turn then slowly tightening up (at a prudent altitude, and not in turbulence). Recover by reducing power and rolling level, recovering from any dive. The worst case scenario would be heavy, with high power and a high turn rate, and it probably best avoided by never getting into a situation where a hard turn or climb is required for safety (i.e. avoiding a bird), because that's when it might happen. The Twinstar (AS 355) has a **LIMIT** light on the caution panel to indicate this condition (the first ones didn't have one, and the swashplate used to get deformed).

In other words, the jacks stall because the blades are stalling and add more and more force to the swashplate, due to the pitching moment of the aerofoil shifting with the stall. When the swashplate gets heavily loaded, it pushes the servos backwards, despite the hydraulic pressure in them (if this were to do with hydraulic pressure, the light would come on first). The feedback forces exert a force equal to the maximum available from the jack so it can no longer move.

On clockwise turning main rotor systems, the right servo receives the highest load when manoeuvring, so servo transparency results in uncommanded right and aft cyclic motion accompanied by down collective movement. The control forces required to counter this aerodynamically induced phenomena are relatively high and could give the impression that the controls are jammed. If you do not reduce the manoeuvre, the aircraft will roll right and pitch-up.

Moral: Don't put an AS 350 in a position where a high G manoeuvre is required to avoid a hard object!

SWITCH FAILURES

The **hydraulic pressure switch** is there to indicate when hydraulic pressure is lost, so that the warning indications (horn and light) can be initiated. SDRs indicate 33 instances of these switches that had to be replaced because they either failed to indicate a pressure loss, or improperly indicated one when the hydraulics were working fine. For example:

"…aircraft suddenly pitched up, controls became stiff. There was no horn of any kind, nor was there any hydraulic pressure drop warning light (HYD light) on warning / caution advisory panel. Pilot continued to evaluate problem, as neared a landing site… Engineer found that hydraulic low pressure switch was defective, vibration caused it into OFF position."

SDR CA030319002, 11/02/02

Here, the hydraulics failed when the pressure switch had already failed and the switch inadvertently turned the hydraulics off through vibration.

SDR searches also reveal 10 instances of malfunctioning **cockpit switches**, ranging from not shutting off the hydraulics to not turning them back on again when selected to ON. There are two involved - the collective mounted Hydraulics Cut-Off Switch and the console-mounted **HYD TEST** switch.

Narratives of the failures of the **collective mounted** switch include:

"During takeoff, aircraft had hydraulic failure. ..hydraulic switch on collective faulty."

SDR 1994110400451*

"Pilot could not turn off hydraulics in flight by pressing button on collective stick. Troubleshooting determined the switch was defective and not supplying voltage to solenoids.

SDR CA0502150009

The switch appears to be able to fail in two ways:

- Uncommanded OFF of the hydraulics
- Not commanding hydraulics OFF

If the switch remains in the Hydraulics ON position, but fails internally, the hydraulic pump will appear to have failed when it has not. There is no choice but to carry out the hydraulics failure procedure in the flight manual, but turning off the hydraulic switch when required will have no effect, as the hydraulics will already be off. You naturally would not notice until you need that facility, as there are no warning signs or symptoms.

The implications of this are that, in normal use, the warning horn associated with a hydraulic failure would also be turned off, so you lose your best warning, although the **HYD** light on the caution panel will come on.

Of course, if the electrics fail, the switches won't work anyway.

© *Phil Croucher, 2011*

AS 355

The AS 355 has two hydraulic systems, each being run by one of the engines, and working through tandem cylinders (that is, the unit contains two servos, back to back), with rotary distributor valves. Having two means that there is always some method of distributing fluid and the control does not jam. The process is controlled by a microswitch.

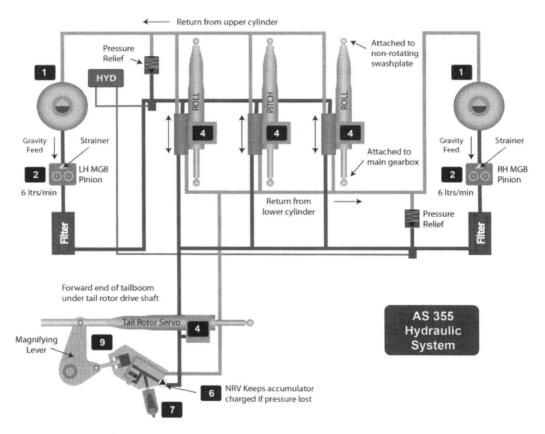

The left hand system supplies the upper cylinders, with the pump being driven by the left hand LH MGB intermediate pinion. The right hand system supplies the lower cylinders, plus the tail rotor servo through an electro valve* (solenoid) that remains open during normal operations. Its purpose is to isolate the tail rotor servo if it seizes (the switch is on the collective).

Both systems supply pressure at 35 bar. The right hand system also has an overload sensor because its roll channel is the most easily stressed, especially during tight manoeuvres in high speed flight. The load sensor causes a **LIMIT** warning light to come on the central warning panel. You should reduce the pitch setting or open out the manoeuvre.

If the left hand system fails, the **HYD** indicator light comes on, but the pedal loads will not change. Therefore if the pedal loads do change, you know that the right hand system has failed.

Note: If the RH system fails in flight, do not press the **ACCU** (**HYD TEST**) button - this increases pedal loads, especially on the right hand side.

*The electro-valve is an electrically actuated device that relieves the high-pressure hydraulic fluid at each servo and the regulator unit, discharging the servos simultaneously.

© *Phil Croucher, 2011*

FUEL

. . . .

The fuel system is designed to provide a supply of clean fuel from the fuel tank to the engine.

The tank is a spin-moulded polyamide fuel cell beneath the transmission deck, containing no baffles. It is non-structural and can tolerate the significant inertial loads and disruption associated with ground impact.

Its capacity is 532 litres (540 for the B2).

The fuel goes through a booster pump at the bottom of the tank (two in the B2), a fuel filter (and filter bypass valve), to the engine-driven fuel pump which supplies fuel to the combustion chamber through a metering unit.

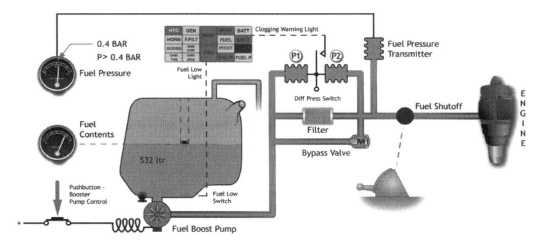

The electric fuel booster pump is water tight and explosion proof, with noise suppression. The motor drives an impeller that draws fuel through a strainer on its way to the engine fuel supply line. An overboard seal drain is provided if there is an internal leak. Regular checks of the seal drain indicate the condition of the dynamic seal.

Once the fuel boost pump is switched on with the pushbutton on the console, its delivery is determined by the demands of the engine (its rated flow is 170 litres per hour). The pressure delivered is inversely proportional to the flow rate, but it never drops below 0.4 bar, which is the yellow arc limit on the fuel pressure gauge. The engine is supplied normally with fuel when the filter is clean and the bypass valve is closed.

Measurement Of Contents

FLOAT SYSTEM

The normal fuel contents transmitter is simply a float that rides vertically in a spiral slot, controlling a potentiometer and a low fuel level switch. The float is free to move with the fuel level, and a pin in its side engages with a slot in the tube wall so that it turns clockwise when it rises and anticlockwise when it descends. A rod transmits the rotation to a magnet at the bottom, which also rotates above a leak proof panel. On the other side, another magnet rotates in sympathy and drives two sliding contact wipers, one of which is connected to the fuel level potentiometer, and the other to the fuel low switch (resistance varies according to the fuel level).

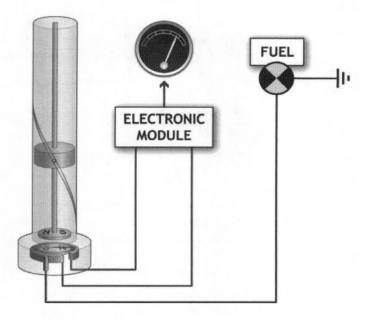

When there is only 60 litres of fuel left in the tank, the wiper grounds the circuit to the **FUEL** warning light, which then comes on.

© *Phil Croucher, 2011*

CAPACITIVE SYSTEM

When this is fitted (as on the B2), 2 concentric electroplated tubes form the plates of a capacitor with either fuel or air acting as the dielectric between them. As the dielectric constant of fuel is twice that of air, the probe capacitance will vary with the fuel level. The signal as measured is sent to the fuel contents indicator via an amplifier.

As the system is DC powered, an inverter is required to make this work, as capacitors do not pass direct current.

A fuel low detector (thermistor) that is connected to another amplifier makes the **FUEL** light come on when 60 litres is remaining in the tank.

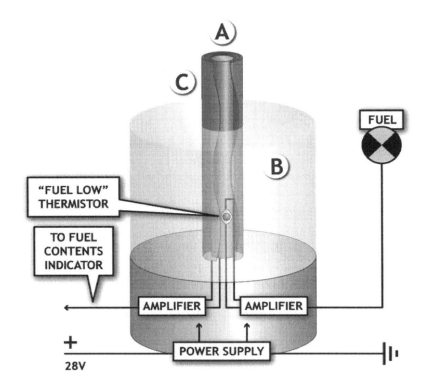

Problems

LOW FUEL PRESSURE

This could be due to:

- Low fuel levels

- Filter Plug

- Low voltage to the pump

LOW FUEL

When there is only 60 litres left in the tank, the low fuel level switch operates the **FUEL** warning light. You have between 20-25 minutes' endurance left.

BOOSTER PUMP FAILURE

The booster pump can deliver 250 litres per hour, at 450 mb. It rotates in one direction only. If it fails (the fuel pressure gauge in the cockpit will read zero), the engine-driven pump can pull fuel from the tank by itself, but you should avoid high-level/high-temperature operations to avoid cavitation (vapour lock*) in the fuel lines.

*Vapour lock occurs when the fuel is allowed to vaporise, and the vapour pressure becomes greater than the fuel system pressure. The fuel supply may get interrupted, and the pump may become unprimed. High temperatures will increase vapour pressure.

The pump has an overboard seal drain that should be checked regularly, as it indicates the condition of the dynamic seal in the pump, and whether there is an internal leak.

FILTER CLOGGING

When impurities build up on the filter cartridge, the flow rate through the filter will reduce, and there will be an increase in the input pressure (P1) and a reduction in the output pressure (P2). The difference will increase in proportion to the clogging, and when it reaches 206 mb, a pressure switch activates the **FILT** warning light, which is amber. This tells you that the bypass is likely to open very soon - 350 ±50 mb, in fact.

The engine will now be supplied with unfiltered fuel, and the fuel control system must be overhauled.

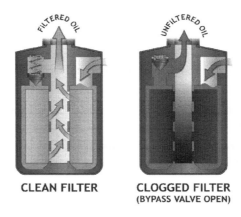

CLEAN FILTER

CLOGGED FILTER
(BYPASS VALVE OPEN)

AS 355

The AS 355 has two tanks, one per engine, tandem mounted (one forward and one rear) below the MGB transmission deck, aft of the cabin bulkhead and between the baggage compartments. The rear one sits slightly higher in the airframe*.

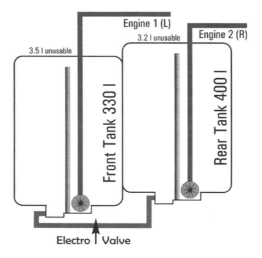

Both are made of aluminium and are an integral part of the cabin structure.

As the batteries are very close to the starboard outboard wall of the rear tank, there is a modification that allows the batteries to be relocated to the forward part of the tailboom so you don't need to use the ballast weights that are often needed to achieve an allowable centre of gravity (useful when you have a well stocked instrument panel). It also gives you more space in the starboard baggage compartment.

The forward tank feeds engine 1 (on the left) and the rear tank feeds engine 2 (on the right). The capacities are 330 ltrs and 400 ltrs, respectively. Unusable fuel is 3.5 and 3.2 ltrs.

You can move fuel from one tank to the other, to keep the quantities of fuel balanced and to allow all the fuel to be used if an engine fails. This is done by gravity, through an electro valve (this takes a LONG time).

The fuel pressure pumps are centrifugal types, with bladed rotors, explosion-proof. The rated delivery is 600 l/hr under 0.8 bar pressure. They maintain pressure at the inlet of the engine pump and bleed the fuel system before starting. If a pump fails, you must fly at a suitable altitude for the fuel to prevent vapour lock. For example, JP5 typically boils out at 6000 feet.

Furl levels are measured with float gauges that are connected indicators graduated in percentage quantities. When the fuel level drops to 6% of the total capacity of both tanks, the **FUEL** light comes on to indicate that around 18 minutes of level flight are remaining.

*Because of the relative positions of the tanks, and their differences in capacity, operating the transfer valve requires certain precautions:

- It must not be opened if the tanks are full, otherwise the forward tank will overflow via the air vent line (the routing of the vent lines stops fuel spilling if the helicopter rolls over).

- If the rear tank is full, there must be less than 40% in the front tank to balance the levels.

- When both tanks are less than 20% full, there will be 4% more in the forward tank. This is to ensure that both engines don't flame out at the same time in the event of fuel starvation.

© *Phil Croucher, 2011*

ELECTRICS

AS 350

There are three potential sources of DC that can supply the busbar that in turn supplies the aircraft circuits:

- A starter-generator supplying 28.5 V/4.8KW. This is the normal power source in flight which also charges the battery. During the start sequence, it is energised by the battery or external power and operates as a motor.

- A battery supplying 24 V/16 Ah. On the ground, it supplies power when the engine is not running, and in flight it provides an emergency supply when the generator fails. Legally, this should be for 30 minutes, but allowing 20 minutes is probably safer.

- An external power unit (which should be detached before flight)

Each source is connected to the busbar through a relay. When the relevant relay is closed, that source can supply the busbar.

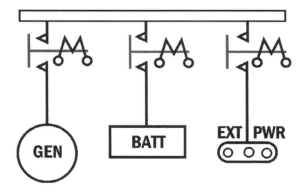

Note: The battery and generator relays can only close when the external power relay is open. The **GEN** and **BAT** warning lights illuminate to indicate the cutting out of the corresponding power source. The **BAT.T** warning light comes on when the battery's internal temperature is over 71°C.

All the above are protected, controlled and monitored through various relays switches and buttons in the Master Equipment Box, which is just forward of the front end of the tailboom.

BUSBARS

From the distribution busbar in the Master Equipment Box, power flows to three busbars that are connected to their various circuits. Each is protected by a thermal circuit breaker.

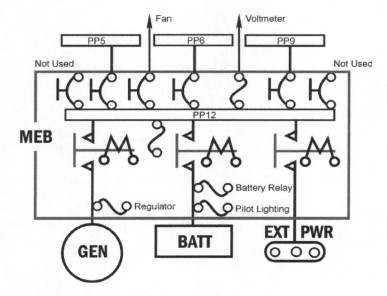

Also connected to the distribution bus is a voltmeter and the engine and main gearbox oil cooling fan. Because the fan has a high current consumption, it has its own circuit breaker.

All other circuits are protected by quick blowing fuses which can be found on two panels in the cockpit, accessible by the pilot in flight.

AC

The AC system supplies 115/26V 400 Hz single phase power for any equipment that needs it, including the autopilot and navigation instruments, through a static inverter.

AS 355

The electrics are a weak point of the AS 355 series, especially in a damp climate. After heavy rain the fire warnings quite often come on until the engines have been running for a while and everything dries out. Moisture also gets into the double electrical emergency cut-off switch, which can stop you from starting up and has caused some unusual failures in flight, depending on which electrical system you have. Also, in heavy rain, if you leave the forward air vent open, rainwater gets in and shorts out the circuit board for the RPM warning system so the horn will come on.

FIRE PROTECTION

Detection

The system can warn you (with a **FIRE** warning light) of any abnormal temperature rises in the engine hot zone, especially at the fuel inlet, oil inlet and outlet, fuel injection ramp, and the engine rear area under the cowling (these points are where detectors are provided).

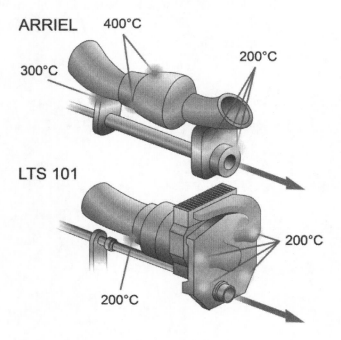

The detectors contain two bimetallic strips, consisting of low- and high-temperature coefficient metals welded together.

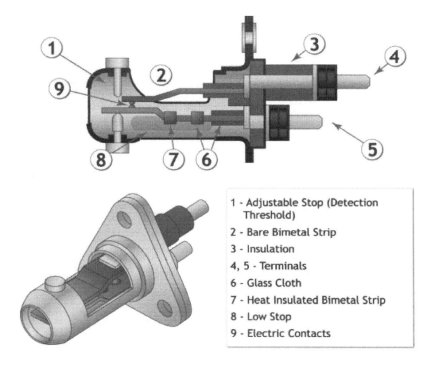

1 - Adjustable Stop (Detection Threshold)
2 - Bare Bimetal Strip
3 - Insulation
4, 5 - Terminals
6 - Glass Cloth
7 - Heat Insulated Bimetal Strip
8 - Low Stop
9 - Electric Contacts

As the temperature rises, one will expand more than the other and bend the assembly enough to make contact with a switch. One bimetallic strip is partially heat insulated with glass-cloth and the other is bare.

In normal circumstances, the electrical contact is closed. Only when temperature increases enough to bend one strip and break the contact does the alarm trigger.

If the temperature rises quickly, the bare strip bends the most and breaks the contact as soon as the threshold is reached. If the temperature rises slowly, both strips will bend at the same rate, but the lower one (which is heat insulated) is longer and runs up against a stop while the bare strip keeps bending, which also breaks the contact.

As the helicopter vibrates naturally, a capacitor is included in the monitoring relay to provide a short time delay and prevent false alarms. The capacitor is normally charged across the relay terminals. As a micro-break occurs, the capacitor discharges and keeps the circuit live for a fraction of a second.

The **FIRE TEST** button cuts the earth return of the monitoring relay.

AUTOMATIC FLIGHT CONTROL

Series actuators in the flight control runs are driven directly by the autopilot computer. The pitch and roll channels also include parallel actuators (trim actuators) that are also connected to the computer through an actuator control unit. The trim actuators move the anchoring point of the cyclic to enhance the limited range of the series actuators.

A sensor (e.g. a gyroscope or a compass) measures the deviation, its amplitude and rate, and outputs a deviation signal. The deviation signal is processed by the computer which generates an appropriate signal for the flight controls.

Actuators

A series actuator is a fast-acting linear mechanical device (usually based around a worm screw) in series with the control run. It gets larger and smaller as required, and moves the aerofoil surfaces for you (any movement in the controls is stopped by the artificial feel system).

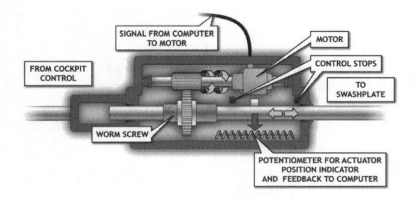

© *Phil Croucher, 2011*

Put more technically, the actuator converts an electrical control into a displacement of its output shaft relative to its body. A neutral position is achieved when the free end of the output shaft is at mid-travel.

In the cockpit, there will be three Actuator Position Indicators (APIs) close together, showing you how the actuators are extending or retracting about their respective mid-points.

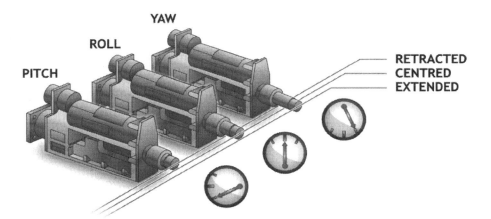

The null meters let you see how hard the series actuators are working and whether or not they are saturated. This is unlikely in pitch and roll, because automatic trims* keep them centred, but it may be observed in yaw control, perhaps after significant power changes, in which case you may have to trim the yaw channel. If you see an indication like the one on the left, you should move the pedals gently to the right.

If the automatic trim fails, you will have to enter the control loop, usually in turbulence, during power changes or when large scale manoeuvres have been commanded. The trim demand light tells you when this is necessary. You centre the relevant API by pressing the trim release button on the cyclic and moving the cyclic in the direction shown by the API pointer. A small amber light below the API comes on whenever its channel is switched off.

*Recentring series actuators needs a lot of effort in terms of attention and control movement. Parallel (trim) actuators are often combined with serial ones to provide a new datum if the series actuators get out of range. On the AS 355, they are also connected to the autopilot computer through an actuator control unit. The trim actuators move the anchoring point of the cyclic to enhance the limited range of the series actuators.

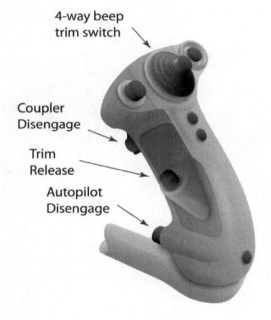

4-way beep
trim switch

Coupler
Disengage

Trim
Release

Autopilot
Disengage

© *Phil Croucher, 2011*

LIMITATIONS & DATA

· ·

T he limitations section of the flight manual contains information that is mandatory.

MEASUREMENTS

· ·

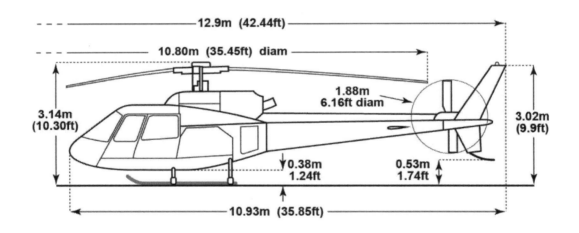

The gross weight limitation of the 350 has a lot to do with controllability when the hydraulics have failed - the B3 has the worst useful load (internally) because of this. The B2 is lighter and the B4 has dual hydraulics and therefore a higher MTOW (2427 kg). Thus, the B3 does not appear to be a significant improvement over a B2, unless you have a specific reason for using one, i.e being hot and high.

LIMITATIONS AND DATA

AS 350

These refer to the basic models - there may be additional restrictions from optional equipment which will be covered by flight supplements in the back of the Flight Manual. As always, the Flight Manual should be checked for the proper figures - these are here for quick reference purposes only.

	B	B1	B2
Max AUW lbs	4300	4850	4961
External Load	4630	5402	5512
Engine	Arriel 1D	Arriel 1D1	
Max alt (feet PA)	16000	20000	20000
Temperature range	-40-+50 C	-40-ISA +35 C	-40-ISA +35 C
Max cargo left (lbs)	264		
Max cargo right (lbs)	220		
Max cargo aft (lbs)	176		
V_{NE} Power on doors closed (mph)*	169	178 at 0 PA	
V_{NE} Power off doors closed (mph)**	138	144 at 0 PA	
V_{NE} doors off (mph)	81	81	
V_{NE} sling load (mph)	92		
Max slope uphill (degs)downhilllateral	1068	1068	1068
Best auto speed (mph)	75		

	B	B1	B2
Rotor RPM - Power On, On ground, low pitch Stabilised flight	375 ± 5 385 ± 5	380 ±5 390±4	380 ±5 390±4
Rotor RPM - Power Off	320-424	320-430	320-430
Max RPM rotor brake			170
Gas generator Max T/O	100 5 mins	100.8 5 mins	
Gas generator Max transient %	105 5 secs	105.5 5 secs	107.5 5 secs
Gas gen Max Cont %	98	98*	98
Max Torque	83	94 above 46 mph 100 below	

	B	*B1*	*B2*
T4 continuous (degs C)	775	795	795
T4 takeoff max (degs C)	810	845	845
T4 trans on start (5 sec)		865	865
T4 startup max (degs C)	840	795	795
Max oil temp (degs C)	110	115	115
Oil pressure min (bars)	1.9	1.8 above 85% NG 1.3 between 70-85%	1.8 > 85% NG 1.3 70-85%
Oil pressure max	10	5 outside start	5 outside start
Normal voltage range	26-29v	26-29v	26-29v
Max voltage	31.5v	31.5v	31.5v
Max current (red line)	150 amps	150 amps	150 amps

*With heating and demisting on, power is limited to 97.5% when OAT is between 0-10 degs C and PA is over 15000 feet.

You can start and stop rotors in winds up to 40 kts from any direction, and 50 kt headwinds. You can hover in 17 kt winds from any direction, and possibly more - up to 30 kts at MAUW has been proven.

FUEL CAPACITIES

Fuel (sg .79)	*Ltrs*	*US gals*	*Imp gals*	*kg*	*lbs*
Total	540	143	119	427	940
Usable after fuel low lt on	60	15.8	13.1	47.4	104
Unusable	1.25	.33	.28	1	2.2

FUEL CONSUMPTION

Consumption is 173 lph for the B, 175 lph for the BA, 190 lph for the B1 and 200 lph for the B2 (each 10% gives you around 0.3). The low fuel light in the B comes on at 15.8 US gals (approx 10-12%). You can use ordinary petrol in emergencies, but only up to 25 hours within any period between overhauls, with a fuel temp up to 30°C. If possible, add 2% of mineral lubricating oil. Refer to the Flight Manual for full details.

The low fuel light in the B comes on at 15.8 US gals (approx 10-12%).

Fuel Type	Jet A-1
Start, taxy and climb	2%, 11 ltrs, 8.7 kg
Normal cruise consumption (each 10% allows around .3)	173 lph (B) 175 lph (BA) 190 lph (B1) 200 lph (B2)
Unusable fuel	11 ltrs, 8.7 kg

OIL CAPACITIES

Mineral and synthetic oils cannot be mixed. Main and tail gearbox synthetic lubricants are Mil-L-7808 or Mil-L-26399. Mineral-based is Mil-L-6086. For the engine, use Mil-L-23699 between -25°C and 50°C. Hydraulics require Mil-H-83282 (synthetic) or 5606 (mineral).

Oil	Ltr	US gal	Imp gal
MGB	6.5	1.7	1.4
TRGB	.33	.08	.07
Engine	6.2	1.64	1.36
Hydraulics	3	.79	.66

AS 355

	F1	*F2*
Max AUW	2400 kg	2540 kg
External Load		
Max alt (PA)	16000 ft	16000 ft
Max cruise power	73% matched Tq or 738 T4	73% matched Tq or 738 T4
Temperature range	-40°C - 35°C	-40°C - 35°C
V_{NE} Power on < 2400 kg		150 kts
V_{NE} Power on >2400 kg		135 kts
V_{NE} Power Off		120 kts
V_{NE} doors off*	70 kts	70 kts
V_{NO}		V_{NE} - 15 kts
Max Torque Transient s/e	112% 6 secs	112% 6 secs
Max Torque continuous twin engine	78%	78%
Min safe climb speed		
Best ROC		
Max Xwind	30 kts	
Max Volts		32
Max Current (per generator)**		150 amps

*Flight with a door off on either side is not approved, except sliding doors.

**Depends on mod state.

Aerobatics and intentional landings in full autorotation are prohibited.

FUEL CAPACITY

Fuel Information			
	Litres	*Kgs*	*%*
Front Tank	333	260	45
Rear Tank	403	317	55
Total	736	577	100

FUEL CONSUMPTION

%	Litres	Kgs	H/Mins
100	730	577	2:55
90	657	519	2:37
80	584	461	2:20
70	511	404	2:02
60	438	346	1:45
55	401.5	317	1:36
50	365	288	1:27
45	328.5	260	1:18
40	292	231	1:10
30	219	173	0:52
20	146	115	0:35
10	73	58	0:17

Fuel Type	Jet A-1
Start, taxy and climb to 2000	5%
Normal cruise consumption	30% per hour*
Unuseable fuel	5 kg
Minimum inflight contents	6%
20 mins at loiter speed	7%
Heating & demisting	6%
Heating & demisting & anti-ice	14%

*Actually 7% per engine per half hour.

OIL CAPACITIES

Oil	Ltr	US gal	Imp gal
MGB	6.5	1.7	1.4
TRGB	.33	.08	.07
Engine	6.2	1.64	1.36
Hydraulics	3	.79	.66

© Phil Croucher, 2011

PERFORMANCE

The information given here is for information purposes only - reference should be made to the relevant flight manual for proper performance information.

AS 350

Generally speaking, for the BA at least, the HIGE graph doesn't even kick in until you're at 1500 ft PA and 40°C (32° OGE). At 30°, start looking in the charts around 3800 feet. The hover height in an AStar is 5 feet.

Picture: AS 350 on sling work

AS 355

F1 vs F2

The F1 and F2 both use the same Allison 250 engines, but the MTOW is higher* on the F2 because you have a bit more power below about 40 knots (about 120 kg). The F2 also has the hydraulic over centre accumulator in the yaw channel so you can keep control if you lose the right hand hydraulic system below the V_{TOSS} of 40 knots..

*The increase is from 2400 to 2540 kgs, although it is only allowed for Performance Class 2 operations.

The maximum weight for Performance Class 1 operations is 2100 kg.

AS 355N

The MAUW on some AS355Ns is 2540kg, and on others it is 2600 kg.

This is due to a modification that involves a few hardware changes (torque gauge, limit light logic, etc.) There is no increase in the power limits though there is a slight advantage for prolonged hovering.

Performance Class 1

Helicopters in this class require no forced landing provisions if the critical power unit fails - the machine can either land within the rejected takeoff distance or continue (safely) to a suitable landing area, depending on when the failure occurs (that is, before or after TDP), clearing all obstacles vertically by 35 feet with an engine out (plus a percentage of DR when IFR), being able to achieve a rate of climb of 100 ft/minute at 200 ft.

In other words, a twin-engined helicopter must be able, if the critical power unit fails at or before TDP, to discontinue the takeoff and to stop within the rejected takeoff area available, or, if the failure occurs at or past TDP, to continue the takeoff and then climb, clearing all obstacles along the flight path by an "adequate margin", which in ICAO-speak is 35 ft.

In addition, there must be the ability to climb to 500 feet above the site at 3% (100 fpm) ROC, and thence to 1000 feet at 1.5%. In the cruise, MOCA must be maintained. For landing, there must be a safe go-around from LDP if a power loss happens or the landing area is compromised, or a safe landing if a power loss occurs after LDP.

© Phil Croucher, 2011

In this way, there should be no chance of an accident if an engine fails *at any stage of a flight*.

There are 2 relevant graphs in the flight manual, depending on the configuration of engine air bleeds.

Note: References to charts in the planning tables below refer to the F1/F2 series.

Enroute

The following performance criteria must be met:

- When out of sight of the surface, the helicopter mass must allow a rate of climb of at least 50 ft/min with OEI at MOCA. Before achieving V_{TOSS} during takeoff, the aircraft must remain clear of cloud and in sight of the surface.

- For day VMC, the calculation of MOCA may allow for obstacles only 900 m on either side of the route to be flown (see later).

Clear Area

TAKEOFF MASS

This is the lesser of weights calculated from:

- The WAT weight for takeoff (FM Supp 11 - Chart 1 or 2)

- The weight allowing a net ROC

- The Rejected Takeoff Space/Takeoff Space required (FM Supplement 11 - Chart 10)

TAKEOFF PROFILE

Refer to the flight manual. TDP is 30 kts & 10 feet.

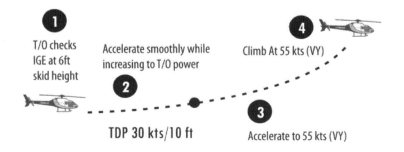

1 — T/O checks IGE at 6ft skid height

Accelerate smoothly while increasing to T/O power

2 — **TDP 30 kts/10 ft**

3 — Accelerate to 55 kts (VY)

4 — Climb At 55 kts (VY)

LANDING MASS

This is the lesser of weights calculated from the following:

- The WAT limit for takeoff
- The Landing Space Required OEI

LANDING PROFILE

Refer to the flight manual. LDP is 40 kts & 100 feet.

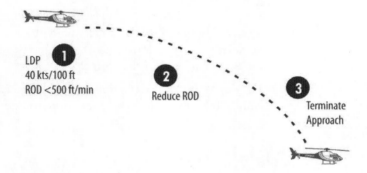

PLANNING TABLE

Criteria	Flight Manual Chart		
Take-off Weight	Chart 1 or 2	RTOW	MAUW
Takeoff Distance Required	Chart 11	TODR	TODA
En-route Climb Weight	Chart 5 or 6	1000 ft	MOCA
Landing Distance Required	Chart 15	LDR	LDA
Landing Weight	Chart 1 or 2	RLW	LW

Helipad

Minimum requirements include a flat firm surface, obstacle-free, at least 27 m across.

TAKE-OFF DISTANCE REQUIRED

If an engine fails immediately after TDP, the helicopter will lose height to gain airspeed, probably down to 35 ft above the helipad, so the area immediately in front of the helicopter must be free from all obstacles above 15 ft in height, out to 100 m and 15° either side of the takeoff path.

TDP is 90 ft above the helipad.

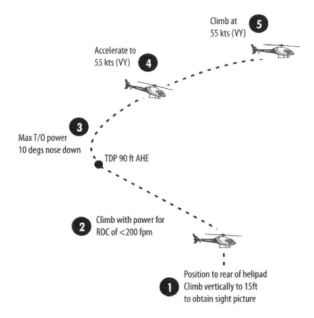

TAKEOFF MASS

The lesser of weights calculated from:

- The WAT weight for takeoff (FM Supplement 11 - Chart 3)

- The weight allowing a net rate of climb defined in para 2.10.1

LANDING MASS

The WAT weight for takeoff (FM Supplement 11 - Chart 3)

LANDING PROFILE

Refer to the Flight Manual. LDP is 30 kts & 90 feet.

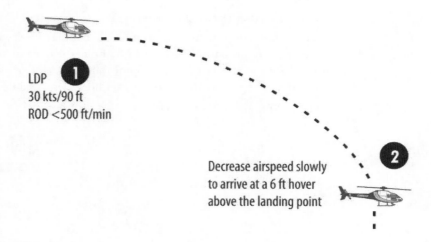

LDP **1**
30 kts/90 ft
ROD <500 ft/min

Decrease airspeed slowly
to arrive at a 6 ft hover
above the landing point

2

PLANNING TABLE

Criteria	Flight Manual Chart		
Take-off Weight	Chart 3	RTOW	MAUW
Takeoff Distance Required		TODR	TODA
En-route Climb Weight	Chart 5 or 6	1000 ft	MOCA
Landing Weight	Chart 1 or 2	RLW	LW

Obstacles

Under JAR OPS 3.477(a), the obstacle domains for Performance Classes 1 & 2 are identical. Obstacles may be disregarded if they are beyond:

- 7R by day, navigating with suitable visual cues

- 10R by night, navigating with suitable visual cues

- 300 m with appropriate navigation aids

- 900 m

Otherwise, those outside the FATO, but within these distances from the intended flight or missed approach paths must be taken account of:

VFR

- Half minimum FATO width, or if none is defined, 0.75D, plus:

- 0.25D (or 3m, whichever is greater), plus:

  - 0.10 DR for day VFR

  - 0.15 DR for night VFR

IFR

For helicopters **shorter than 15 m**, the greater of 30 m or 1½ D, plus:

- 0.10 DR with **accurate course guidance** (ILS)

- 0.15 DR with **standard course guidance** (ADF, VOR)

- 0.3 DR with **no course guidance**

There must be no turns of more than 15° change of direction below 200 feet (61m). Under JAR OPS 3.495, turns more than 15° need an extra "adequate margin" to be allowed vertically - under ICAO, this usually means 35 ft. The divergence of the obstacle accountability area only applies after the end of the TODA.

Obstacle Avoidance

Not to scale!!

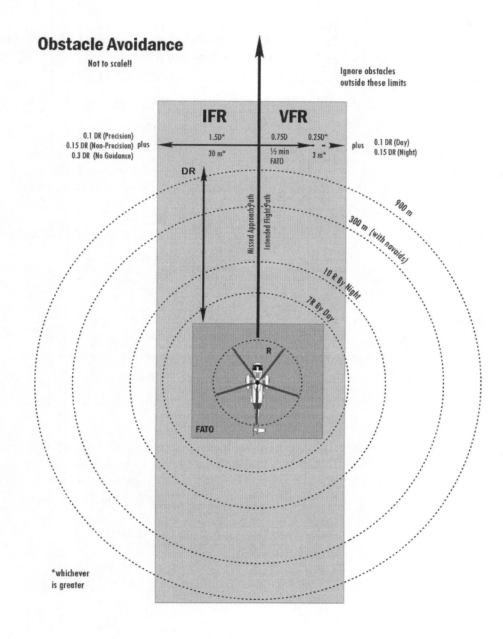

Ignore obstacles
outside these limits

IFR **VFR**

0.1 DR (Precision)
0.15 DR (Non-Precision) plus
0.3 DR (No Guidance)

1.5D*   0.75D   0.25D*
30 m*   ½ min   3 m*
         FATO

plus   0.1 DR (Day)
        0.15 DR (Night)

DR

Missed Approach Path   Intended Flight Path

900 m
300 m (with novaids)
10 R By Night
7R By Day

R

FATO

*whichever
is greater

WEIGHT & BALANCE

The details given here should be verified with those in the Flight Manual.

AS 350

The longitudinal C of G starts at 124.8" aft of datum up to 4429 lbs, after which it reduces to 126" at 4850 lbs MAUW. The aft limit is 137.8" to 2646 lbs, changing to 135"at MAUW. The Datum is -133.8" forward of the main rotor head centreline. Lateral C of G limits are from 7.08" left to 5.51" right in the B (the machines are different). Be aware that, for the BA, the C of G graph for the cargo sling (or swing) indicates a maximum weight of 4960 lbs, as opposed to the 4988 lbs on the front of the supplement.

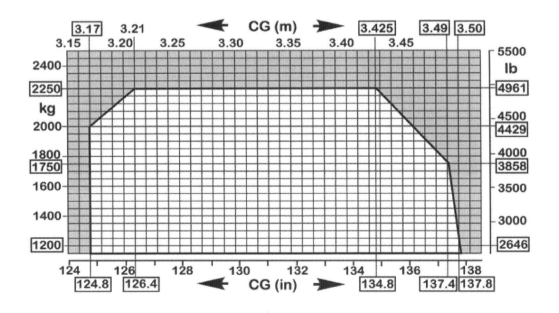

The MAUW is 4950 lbs because safe flying above that weight could not be demonstrated without hydraulics.

Loading Considerations

Seat belt anchor points can be used to secure freight in the passenger cabin. Cargo tie downs are fitted in the cabin floor, each having a 1000 kg capacity. The maximum floor loading is 600 kg/m^2.

When passengers and freight are carried together, freight should be stowed and secured so that it does not impede door or liferaft access.

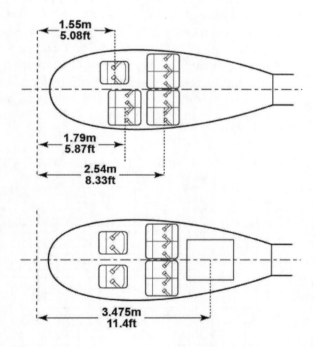

BAGGAGE HOLD LIMITS

Luggage Hold	Maximum Load
Max load rear baggage bay	80 kgs
Max load Port baggage bay	100 kgs
Max load Starboard baggage bay	120 kgs

AS 355

The longitudinal C of G starts at 124.8" aft of datum up to 2000 kg, after which it reduces to 127.9" at 2500 kg MAUW. The aft limit is 139.3" to 2100 kg, changing to 135.8"at MAUW. The Datum is -133.8" forward of the main rotor head centreline, and is the symmetry plane. Lateral C of G limits are from 6.30" left to 3.54" right.

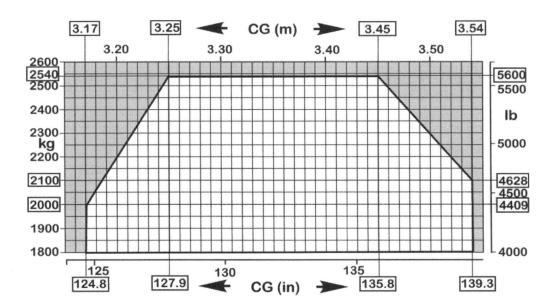

Loading Considerations

Seat belt anchor points can be used to secure freight in the passenger cabin. Cargo tie downs are fitted in the cabin floor, each having a 1000 kg capacity. The maximum floor loading is 600 kg/m^2.

When passengers and freight are carried together, freight must be stowed and secured so that it does not impede door or liferaft access.

The only items moving the C of G aft are fuel in the rear tank and cargo or baggage in the rear hold. When more than four passengers are carried, it is possible that the forward C of G will be exceeded unless a compensating weight is placed in the rear hold. This is particularly important with shuttle or pleasure flights. The rear baggage hold should be used first and the side holds only if the rear hold bulks out.

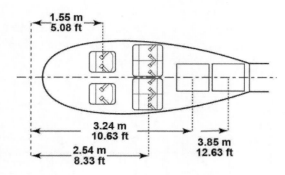

BAGGAGE HOLD LIMITS

Luggage Hold	Maximum Load
Max load rear baggage bay	80 kgs
Max load Port baggage bay	100 kgs
Max load Starboard baggage bay	120 kgs

WEIGHING THE AIRCRAFT

Three jacking points are used:

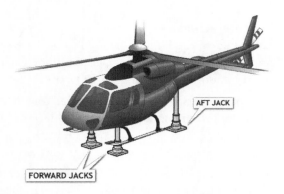

© *Phil Croucher, 2011*

CHECKLISTS

9

The standard checks in the flight manual are nowhere near good enough for commercial air transport - the suggested ones listed below have been based on experience, with emphasis on doing as much as possible before turning the battery on.

In general, check moveable parts, metal and wiring (as applicable) for lubrication, servicing, security of attachment, binding, excessive wear, security, proper operation and adjustment, correct travel, cracked fittings, security of hinges, defective bearings, cleanliness, corrosion, deformation, sealing, condition of paint and tension. In particular, check the cowling security, as many hinges are flimsy (especially the 355), and the bolts that secure the rear door at the top and bottom on each side.

If the aircraft has been grounded for more than a week, wipe the servo control piston rods with a rag dampened with hydraulic fluid.

AS 350

Preflight/Daily Check

Remove engine blanking plates and fuselage/blade covers. Ensure that the area is clear, external power and fire extinguishers are available, frost, ice, slush and snow is removed (particularly on upper surfaces of rotor blades, aerials, air intakes/outlets and undercarriage). Inspect the cabin for loose articles and check seat assemblies and seat belts for satisfactory condition, locking and release.

The First Aid kit should be securely stowed and the fire extinguisher fully charged, in date and in their appointed places. Doors should have exit signs inside and outside with opening instructions for handles (2 on each door).

CABIN

1 Controls. . . . . Check for free travel

2 Instruments, switches and controls . . . . Check for signs of damage

3 Altimeter . . . . Check and set to airfield elevation, accuracy

4 Battery . . . . Switch on. Fuel quantity should agree with tank

5 Landing, nav lights and pitot heat . . . . .Check operation

6 Battery . . . . Switch Off

7 Pitot head . . . . .Check for cleanliness

8 Sideslip indicator . . . . Release, check wool free

9 Windows . . . . Cleanliness, cracking, security

10 Wiper. . . . . .Check for freedom

RIGHT HAND SIDE FUSELAGE

1 Cabin door . . . Check for cleanliness, security, hinge pins, door seal and
. . . . jettison

2 OAT gauge . . . . Check

3 Transmission air duct clear. . . . . Check

4 Static vents . . . . Free of ice and clean

5 Belly panels . . . . Secure, condition

6 Belly aerials . . . . Secure, condition

7 Landing gear . . . . Secure, condition

8 Battery attachment (inside compartment) . . . . Secure

9 Baggage hold door . . . . Secure

10 Landing gear shock strut . . . . Secure, no leaks

11 Ground power receptacle. . . . . .Closed

12 Lower fairing panels . . . . Secure

13 MGB & engine cowlings . . . .Open and check condition & cleanliness,
. MGB suspension strut, servos and lines & mast bearing magnetic plug,
engine oil tank and system for level, attachment and leaks, hydraulic and
. . . . gearbox oil levels, engine support, engine and compartment

14 MGB & engine cowlings . . . . .Close

CARGO HOOK

Check the electrical and mechanical release mechanisms by watching the hook open correctly. With the electrical system unarmed, make sure the hook does *not* release when the release button is pressed.

1 Release lever on hook. . . . . Operation
2 Cargo hook load beam . . . . Damage and wear
3 Load retention latch . . . . . Freedom, operation of return spring, damage
4 Hook and swing frame . . attachment (cotter and pip pins) and condition
5 Suspension cables and bungees . . . . Condition and fraying
6 Elastomer stop on cargo swing arm . . . . Ensure correct position
. . . . to prevent damage to electrical connectors on hook
7 Electrical connectors . . . . Fraying, etc
8 Manual emergency release cable . . . . . Condition of exposed length, and sheath
9 Quick disconnect . . . safetied and securely attached to mounting clip on airframe

RHS TAILBOOM

1 Oil leaks . . . . None under scuppers
2 Horizontal stabiliser . . . . . . Cracks on skin within 50mm of attachment.
. . . . Check play
3 Tailboom and TGB fairings, tail rotor drive shaft . . . . Security
4 Vertical fins . . . . Condition
5 Tailrotor gearbox . . . . Oil levels, sealing, chip plug, cowlings for security
6 Drive shaft cover . . . . Damage, securty
7 Tail boom . . . . Condition, damage

TAIL ROTOR

In general, check blade skin condition, bonding separation, scratches, cracks, dents and deformation. Check polyurethane protective strips on blade roots and impact-indicating finger on blade tips. On stainless steel leading edges, no perforation or debonding. Check elastomers for metal showing.

1 Blades . . . . .push back & forth, listen for abnormal noise at root . . . . (broken fibres)

2 Laminated half-bearings . . . . delaminations, cracks or protrusions

3 Tail rotor head, pitch change rods . . . . .Check for axial play

4 Pitch change spider bearing . . . . Check for play

5 Tail rotor gearbox . . . . Security, bellcrank hinge pin

6 Sealing head . . . . .Check abnormal play

7 See-saw hinge teetering bearings . . . . Check for cracks in rubber . . . . on bearing outer zone

8 Control Spider . . . . . Baffles, spacers and lock washers should not rotate

LHS TAILBOOM

As for right hand side.

LEFT HAND SIDE FUSELAGE

1 Baggage hold door . . . . Operation
2 Fuel cap. . . . . On and secure
3 Fuel . . . . Drain samples
4 Landing gear leg . . . . Check at top for impact with body (hard landings)
5 MGB cowlings . . . . .Open & check as for RHS
6 Transmission deck and engine compartment . Condition and cleanliness
7 Lower fairing panels. . . . . .Security, damage
8 Main rotor head . . . . .Check:
. . . . Star, sleeves (peeling)
. . . . .Frequency Adapter for crack debonding and separation
. . . . .Spherical Thrust bearing for blistering, separation, cracks
. . . . .Swashplate assembly, for grease, overheating and feel
. . . . .Pitch Change Rods-cup movement, paint marks aligned
. . . . Main Rotor Shaft
. . . . .MGB suspension strut
. . . . .Servo units and hydraulic system for security and leaks
. Main Rotors - check for security, signs of impact, earthing straps secure
9 Engine Air Intake. . . . . Clear
10 Engine Cowling . . . . . Open and check engine mount & compartment

Prestart

1. Doors . . . . Shut
2. Extinguisher . . . . Secure
3. Harness . . . . Fastened
4. Cyclic . . . . Set Neutral
5. Cyclic Friction . . . . On
6. Pedals . . . . Neutral
7. Collective . . . . Latched
8. Heater . . . . Off

Tip: Crack the ventilators open slightly, so if any leaking hydraulic gets sucked into the engine, you can smell it before the light comes on).

9. Rotor Brake . . . . Off (Fwd)
10. Fuel Flow Lever . . . . Off (Rear)
11. Fuel Shut Off . . . . Wire Locked Fwd
12. Battery . . . . On
13. Gen . . . . On
14. Fuel Pump . . . . On 30 Secs
. . . . Check Pressure
15. Warning Lights . . . . Test
16. Anti-Collision . . . . On
17. Avionics . . . . Off
18. Fuel Pressure . . . . Check
19. Battery Volts . . . . Check
20. Fuel Quantity . . . . Note
21. Captions . . . . Lit

Start

After 30 seconds Boost.

1. Starter Button . . . . Press
2. Ng. . . . . Rising
3. 10% Ng . . . . Fcl 1/3 Open
4. T4 . . . . Control Within 600-700
5. Rotor . . . . Turning By 19% Ng
6. 40-45% Ng. . . . . Release Starter Button
7. FCL . . . . Fwd Gate(Tq Below 30%)
8. Caption Out. . . . . Mgb.P
. . . . Eng.P (70%Ng)
. . . . Hyd Off
. . . . Horn Light On
9. FCL . . . . In Fwd Gate
10. Nr . . . . 370-380 Rpm

ABORTING START

1. FCL . . . . Close
2. Fuel Pump . . . . Off
3. Gen. . . . . Off
. . . . "Crank" Engine

If A High T4 Abort

4. Check Batt Voltage
5. Batt Voltage Ok. . . . . "Crank" 15 Secs.
. . . . Then Attempt Re-Start
6. Move FCL Slowly . . . . Check No Ng Drop

AFTER START

1. Horn.. On, Light Out
2. Pitot Heat...................................... On, Light Out
3. Cyclic Friction .... Off

Hyd. Accumulator Check

4. Press Hyd Test........................ Hyd Lights, Horn On
5. 4 Cyclic Circles 2" ....No Increase In Loading
6. Press Hyd Test (Off)......................Hyd Out, Horn Off

Hyd Pressure Isolation Check

7. Switch Off ....Hyd Light On/Load Increase
8. Switch On ....Horn Off/Hyd Light Out
.... (2-3 Secs.)
9. Avionics ....On

Pre Takeoff

1. Ammeter .... Check
2. Engine Oil Pressure.................................. Check
3. Fuel Pressure .... Check
4. Voltage 28v
5. Fuel Contents.....................................Sufficient
6. Torque c20%
7. Ng..c82%
8. T4 .... Within Limits
9. Warning Lights (Except Bleed Valve)...................... Out
10. Instruments ....Set
11. Friction..Adjust
12. Heater.. Off
13. Harness' / Doors....................................Secure
14. Strobe Light ....On
15. Position Lights................................... As Required
16. Wind Check .... Strength / Direction
17. Lookout

After Takeoff

1. Nr . . . . Normal
2. Torque . . . . Check
3. T's & P's . . . . Within Limits

Shutdown

1. Collective . . . . Latched
2. Cyclic Friction . . . . On
3. Horn. . . . . Off
4. Fuel Pump . . . . Off
5. Pitot Heat. . . . . Off
6. Avionics Etc. . . . . Off
7. FCL . . . . Set 67-70% For 30 Secs.
. . . . Then Off (Rear)
8. Generator. . . . . Off
9. Rotor Brake . . . . Apply Below 140 Rpm
10. Battery . . . . Off

When Rotor Has Stopped, Unlatch Collective To Reduce Stress On
Starflex

11. Aircraft. . . . . Secure As Required:
. . . . Doors Locked, Rotor Brake Applied & Rotor Blades Tied Down

After Last Flight

This check maintains airworthiness, and is similar to the Daily Check, with some items due on the 30-hour being done on the nearest ALF (After Last Flight check), and others that need particular attention (in bold). Also check the Tech Log for defects, etc.

CABIN EXTERIOR

1 Transparent panels . . . . cleanliness, clean as required

2 Pitot & static vents . . . blockage, damage and security - install protective . . . . covers

3 Sideslip indicator wool . . . . Check for condition

4 Door jambs, canopy arch members. . . . . no defects or cracks

5 LHS cabin door . . . . Closed and latched

6 Sliding windows . . . . . Defects, cracks, bonding separation, loss of slide

7 LHS baggage compartment . . . . Cargo secured, door condition . . . . and securely latched

8 LHS landing gear crosstube and skid. . . . . . . .Condition, shock for leaks . . . . and wear plates on landing gear skid tubes for condition

9 Main transmission. . . . . . . .Condition of locking systems, check oil level . . . . .and condition of electric chip plug wire, ... check deck for cleanliness and leaks

10 Upper bearing face of laminates . . . . .Check for cracks . . . . (for bi-directional cross beams pre-mod 072720)

11 Main transmission. . . . . .Check suspension bars for security

12 Servos . . . . Check for security and leakage . . . . (particularly Dunlop ones for cracks in the body)

13 Hydraulic system. . . . Check for security, condition of lines and unions, ... no leakage, and hydraulic reservoir for fluid level and attachment

14 Cooling fan motor . . . . Check for security and condition of blades

15 Small fuel filter . . . . Check for alignment of index mark, ... clogging indicator not visible, safetying of filter bowl lock wire

16 Main transmissions to engine liaison tube universal joint pins . . . . Check for security, diaper pins in place, locked and tie wrapped

17 Main rotor swashplate bearing. . . . . . Check within 5 minutes of rotors
. . . . stopping for abnormal heat when touched, no grease runs,
. . . . .discolouration and flaking of paint.

18 Scissors, swashplate bearing, rod ends and swivel bearings . . . . . Check
. . . . for condition, security and increased play

19 Interface between swashplate and pitch change rod end fittings. Check
. . for signs of contact and paint scaling on swashplate attachment yokes

20 Pitch change rod end fittings . . . . Check for condition and
. . . . no radial play in bearing ends. Paint marks on the bearing ends
. . . . (post mod 076110, 076159 and 076165) must be visible and aligned

21 Visible sections of the main rotor shaft . . . . Check for paint condition,
. . . no dents, scratches, cracks, crazing, blistering, corrosion, tool marks,
. . . . particularly under the hub

22 Main rotor hub . . . . Check for security and general condition
. . . . Check star for delamination (splinters) or cracks
. . . . Check star recesses for cracks

23 Spherical thrust bearings & frequency adapters . No elastomer defects,
. . . . . . bonding separation, fissures, blisters, extrusion or cracks allowed

24 Two-layer frequency adapter . . . . Check for clearance between
. . . . adapter and metal shim

25 Self-lubricating bearings . . . . .Check for debris or play

26 Bushes in ends of Starflex hub arms . . . . There should be no space
. . . . between the adhesive bead and the bush

27 Flared housing magnetic plug . . . . Check for metal chips

28 Anti-vibrator . . . . Check for security

29 Main rotor blades . . . . .Check for security, general skin condition,
. . . . .tabs and polyuethane protective strips on blade roots
. . . . Visually check for bonding separation, scratches, cracks,
. . . . dents and deformation of blades. Check no perforation on
. . . . .stainless steel leading edge protective strips,
. . . . none due to erosion, no debonding, no dents

30 Transmission cowl . . . . Close, ensure latches are locked

31 Aft baggage compartment . . . . Check door closed and securely latched

TAIL BOOM LHS

1 LHS . . . . Check for damage

2 LHS horizontal stabiliser . . . . .Condition and security

3 Navigation light . . . . Condition

4 Tail rotor drive shaft cover. . . . . .Security

5 **B3 only** . . . - Check the forward tail rotor driveshaft cover and attached
. . . . . . heatshield for condiion and cracks, particularly around the 6-side
. . . . attachment points on the fairing. Use a mirror if necessary

TAIL ROTOR

1 Upper and lower vertical fin. . . . . . . .Damage, security & working rivets

2 Tail skid. . . . . .Security and condition

3 Tail rotor guard. . . . . If installed, check for security and condition

4 Tail cone fairing . . . . Check for security

5 Tail light lens & bulb . . . . .Check for condition

6 Tail rotor gearbox. . . . . .Check for:
. . . . .Security of gearbox (apply load on output driveshaft)
. . . . Pitch control bellcrank mounting yoke blend radius for cracks
. . . . Bellcrank pivot bolt for play
. . . . Sealant bead around bolt for condition
. . . . Oil level and leaks
. . . . Magnetic plug for metal accumulation

7 Tail rotor swashplate . . . . . . .Check for alignment of black index marks
. . . . on rotating plate and spacer

8 Tail rotor blades . . . . Check as follows:
. . . . .Skins for condition, bonding separation, scratches,
. . . . .cracks, dents and deformation
. . . . Polyurethane protective strips on blade roots
. . . . Impact-indicating finger on blade tips
. . . . No perforation on stainless steel leading edge protective strips
. . . . from erosion, no debonding upper & lower faces

9 Tail rotor blade spar . . . . . .Check for abnormal noise by flapping blades . . . . .towards and away from the tail boom . . . .- maximum required is 4 inches or 10 cm

10 Laminated half-shell bearings . . .Check for bonding separation, cracks

11 Blade horns. . . . . .Inspect for play

12 Tail rotor yoke to shaft mating areaCheck security, condition of sealant

13 Tail rotor pitch change links . . . . . . .Check for play by imparting a low . . . . amplitude see-saw motion to the blades.

14 Spider swivel bearing .Check visually for no extrusion of Teflon fabric, ... disclouration and and/or scoring on the ball

15 See-saw (flapping) hinge . . . . Check according to type:
    Type 1 Early Laminated: Cups on either side of pin for necessary play
    Type 2 Spherical: Flappng bearings - no play
    Type 3 Current Laminated: No cracks, rubber extrusion, bronze chips

16 Freewheel . . . . Check for proper operation from the tail rotor
    When the tail rotor is turned clockwise, the free turbine should turn.
    When the tail rotor is turned counter-clockwise, the free turbine
    should desynchronise and not turn.

TAIL BOOM RHS

1 RHS of tail boom. . . . . Check for damage

2 RHS horizontal stabiliser .Condition and security

3 RHS navigation light . . . . .Damage

4 Tail rotor drive shaft cover . . . . Security

5 Tail boom skin . .Inspect for cracks in the developing from the last rivet
    attachment hole of aerodynamic strake

RHS FUSELAGE

1 Battery . . . . Security and signs of leakage

2 RHS baggage compartment door. . . . . Condition, securely latched

3 RHS landing gear crosstube and skid . . . Condition, shock for no leaks, ... wear plates on landing gear skid tubes

4 Transmission cowl . . . Open, check transmission & deck for cleanliness . . . . & signs of leaks

5 Transmission. . . . . Check magnetic plug for metal chips

6 Hydraulic system. . . . . . Check for security, condition of lines & unions, ...no leakage

7 Hydraulic pump belt. . . . . Condition

8 Hydraulic filter/valve assembly clogging indicator. . . . Check not visible . . . . .If it is extended, replace filter cartridge

9 Servos . . . . Check for security and leakage . . . . Check Dunlops for cracks in body which could cause seepage

10 Main transmission bars. Security and condition
For **bi-directional crossbeams pre-mod 072720**, check for cracks in upper bearing face of laminates.

11 Engine oil tank . . Check for correct oil level and security, cap installed

12 Engine oil cooler. . . . . .Check for security and no leaks

13 Main transmission to engine Liaison Tube universal joint pins . . Check security, diaper pins in place, ends locked and pins tie wrapped in pairs

14 Engine cowling . . . . Open, check condition of latching systems

15 Engine air intake area . . . . .Check clear of foreign matter, ...and ice or snow accumulation

16 Seal between engine air intake duct and underside of engine cowling . . . . .Check condition

17 Engine air intake duct. . . . . Check for security

18 Engine, accessories and compartment. . . . . Check for condition, ...cleanliness and leakage

19 Accessories and piping . . . . Check for signs of wear from . . . . .insufficient clearance between pipes and engine parts

20 Electric equipment and harness attachments (connector locking). . . . . .Check condition

21 N_F/N_G controls. . . . Interference and security of rod end connections

22 Front engine mount (M01 to Liaison Tube adapter) . .Check for cracks
. . . . .and signs of oil leakage from the output shaft magnetic seal

23 Aft engine mount . . . . .Check for security and signs of looseness

24 RHS and LHS engine deck drains . . . . Not plugged

25 Exhaust pipe. . . . . Check for condition, cracks and security

26 Axial compressor wheel. . .Check for damage on the leading edges and
free rotation of the compressor assembly, no abnormal rub noise

27 During engine shutdown, after the last flight, listen for unusual noises

28 When T4 is less than 150°C, (approx 30 minutes after shutdown),
crank the engine for a *maximum* of 5 seconds and check there is no
rubbing noise during gas generator rundown. You can also rotate the
gas generator by hand through the engine inlet. Ensure the compressor
rotates freely without rubbing.

29 Inspect the freewheel unit for correct operation by rotating the blades
of the free turbine from inside the exhaust pipe. From the rear, the free
turbine should disengage counter-clockwise and drive the main rotor
when turned clockwise

30 Check for leaks on the rear bearing oil ducts

31 Oil filter impending bypass indicator . Checkfor popped indicating pin

32 Reduction gear (M05) magnetic plug (pre-mod TU232) . . . . Check

33 Module mating flanges Tightness, signs of oil or high pressure oil leaks

34 Outer casings of combustor, free turbine, and exhaut diffuser (exhaust
pipe attachment) . . . . Check for freedom from cracks

35 If the aircraft has the optional cycle-counting unit, carry out a
coherence check and recording of cycles

36 Magnetic plugs:

    No metal chips on forward plug (accessory gearbox, M01) (optional)

    No metal chips on aft plug (reduction gearbox, M05)

    Aft reduction gear magnetic plug pre-TU 135 check daily

    Post-mod TU 135

37 Engine cowl . . . . .Close, check for correct locking of latches

38 Inlet and exhaust covers. . . . . Install

AS 355

External Check

Remove engine blanking plates and fuselage/blade covers. Ensure that the area is clear, external power and fire extinguishers are available, frost, ice, slush and snow is removed (particularly on upper surfaces of rotor blades, aerials, air intakes/outlets and undercarriage). Inspect the whole of the cabin for loose articles and check all seat assemblies and seat belts for satisfactory condition, locking and release. The First Aid kit should be securely stowed and the fire extinguisher fully charged, in date and in its appointed place. Both items should be signed as checked and dated.

Each door should have an exit sign inside and outside with opening instructions for each handle (2 on each door). The Flight Manual should be under a seat, with other items, like cloths, windscreen cleaner etc., and the Ops Manual. Lifejackets should be under the rear seats, and safety cards and sick bags are required as well. There should be a full complement of headsets or ear defenders.

1 Controls. . . . . Check for free travel

2 Instruments, switches and controls . . . . Check for signs of damage

3 Altimeter . . . . Check and set to airfield elevation, accuracy within ±50'

4 Battery . . . . Switch on. Fuel quantity should agree with tank

5 Landing, nav lights and pitot heat . . . . .Check operation

6 Battery. . . . . Switch Off

7 Pitot head . . . . .Check for cleanliness

8 Sideslip indicator . . . . Release, check wool free

9 Windows . . . . Cleanliness, cracking, security

10 Wiper. . . . . .Check for freedom

Right Hand Side Fuselage

1 Cabin door . . . Check for cleanliness, security, hinge pins, door seal and jettison

2 OAT gauge . . . . Check

3 Transmission air duct clear. . . . . Check

4 Static vents . . . . Free of ice and clean

5 Belly panels . . . . Secure, condition

6 Belly aerials . . . . Secure, condition

7 Landing gear . . . . Secure, condition

8 Battery attachment (inside compartment) . . . . Secure

9 Baggage hold door . . . . Secure

10 Landing gear shock strut . . . . Secure, no leaks

11 Ground power receptacle . . . . Closed

12 Lower fairing panels . . . . Secure

13 MGB & engine cowlings . . . . Open and check:

    Condition and cleanliness

    MGB suspension strut, servo units & lines & mast bearing mag plug

    Engine oil tank and system for level, attachment and leaks

    Hydraulic and gearbox oil levels

    Fire extinguisher pressure

    Engine support

    Engine and compartment

14 MGB & engine cowlings . . . . Close

Cargo Hook

Check the electrical and mechanical release mechanisms by watching the hook open correctly. With the electrical system unarmed, make sure the hook does *not* release when the release button is pressed.

1 Release lever on hook . . . . Operation

2 Cargo hook load beam . . . . Damage and wear

3 Load retention latch . . . . . Freedom, operation of return spring, damage

4 Hook and swing frame . . attachment (cotter and pip pins) and condition

5 Suspension cables and bungees . . . . Condition and fraying

6 Elastomer stop on cargo swing arm . . . . Ensure correct position

. . . . to prevent damage to electrical connectors on hook

7 Electrical connectors . . . . Fraying, etc

8 Manual emergency release cable   Condition of exposed length, & sheath

9 Quick disconnect . . . safetied and securely attached to mounting clip on airframe

RHS Tailboom

1 Oil leaks . . . . None under scuppers

2 Horizontal stabiliser Cracks on skin within 50mm of attachment. Check play

3 Tailboom and TGB fairings, tail rotor drive shaft . . . . Security

4 Vertical fins . . . . Condition

5 Tailrotor gearbox . . . Oil levels, sealing, chip plug, cowlings for security

6 Drive shaft cover . . . . Damage, securty

7 Tail boom . . . . Condition, damage

Tail Rotor

Check blade skin condition, bonding separation, scratches, cracks, dents and deformation. Check of polyurethane protective strips on blade roots and impact-indicating finger on blade tips. On stainless steel leading edges, no perforation or debonding. Check elastomers for metal showing.

1 Blades . . push back and forth, listen for abnormal noise at root (broken fibres)

2 Laminated half-bearings . . . . delaminations, cracks or protrusions

3 Tail rotor head, pitch change rods . . . . Check for axial play

4 Pitch change spider bearing . . . . Check for play

5 Tail rotor gearbox . . . . Security, bellcrank hinge pin

6 Sealing head . . . . Check abnormal play

7 See-saw hinge teetering bearings . Check for cracks in rubber on bearing outer zone

8 Control Spider . . . . . Baffles, spacers and lock washers should not rotate

LHS Tailboom

As for right hand side.

Left Hand Side Fuselage

1 Baggage hold door . . . . Operation
2 Fuel cap. . . . . On and secure
3 Fuel . . . . Drain samples
4 Landing gear leg . . . . Check at top for impact with body (hard landings)
5 MGB cowlings . . . . .Open & check as for RHS
6 Transmission deck and engine compartment . Condition and cleanliness
7 Lower fairing panels. . . . . .Security, damage
8 Main rotor head . . . . .Check:

  Star, sleeves (peeling)
  Frequency Adapter for crack debonding and separation
  Spherical Thrust bearing for blistering, separation, cracks
  Swashplate assembly, for grease, overheating and feel
  Pitch Change Rods-cup movement, paint marks aligned
  Main Rotor Shaft
  MGB suspension strut
  Servo units and hydraulic system for security and leaks
  Main Rotors - check security, signs of impact, earthing straps secure

9 Engine Air Intake. . . . . Clear
10 Engine Cowling . . . . . Open and check engine mount & compartment

Prestart

1 Hatches/Harnesses. . . . . Secure
2 Controls, pedals . . . . Adjusted, collective locked
3 Landing lights . . . . Off
4 Engine anti-ice . . . . Off
5 Cabin Heat . . . . Off, open slightly
6 Standby Static Switch . . . . Normal
7 Direct Battery Switch . . . . On, light illuminated
8 Instruments. . . . . Check
9 Switches (Horn, pitot, generators, etc) . . . . Off
10 Battery. . . . . On, check voltage
11 Anti-collision light . . . . .On
12 Fuel contents. . . . . Check sufficient
13 Fuel tank crossfeed. . . . . Off
14 Warning panel. . . . . Test - inc fire (1 sec delay). Check these lights:
. . .GEN LH, GEN RH, HORN, PITOT, HYD RH, HYD LH, ENG P,
. . . . MGB P, SERVO
15 Servo . . . . Test, light out
16 Auto Relight . . . . Test, then cancel
17 Electrical Status Switch . . . . V Ess
18 Fuel Control Levers . . . . .Aft
19 Fuel shut off levers. . . . . .Forward, safety wired
20 Rotor brake . . . . Off (fully forward)

Start

1 Area and rotors . . . . Clear

2 Fuel boost 1st engine . . . . .On, check pressure

3 Starter button . . . . Engage

4 Throttle . Open at 15% N_1 and TOT <150°C. Check engine oil pressure rising, blades turning. Modulate as required to maintain T4

5 Starter . Release at 60% N_1. Run for 1 min if engine has been shut down over 15 mins

6 Auto relight. . . . . .Press to extinguish light

7 Throttle . . Forward to flight idle. GEN/HYD/MGB P/SERVO out by N_R 200. HORN light flashes between 250-360 N_R, steady above 360

8 Generator . . . . .On

9 Second engine. . . . . Start as above, check both generators on

After Start

1 External Power. . . . . Disconnect

2 Volts, Amps . . . . Checked

3 Ts and Ps. . . . . .Within limits

4 Instruments, radios. . . . . On, checked

5 Radios/Navaids . . . . .As required (all panels)

6 Pitot Heat, Horn. . . . . On, light out

7 Hydraulic Yaw Servo . . . . Test, check load

8 Aural warning . . . . On, light out

Pre Takeoff

1 Ts and Ps . . . . .Within limits
2 Warning panel, Auto lts . . . . Out
3 Throttles, etc . . . . 5 levers full forward, N_R 390 +4, -5
4 Control frictions . . . . Adjusted
5 Heat/Demist . . . . As required
6 Anti-col/Position lights . . . . .On
7 Landing light . . . . As required
8 Float pin . . . . As required
9 Flight Instruments . . . . Set
10 Radios, transponder . . . . Set
11 Anti-icing . . . . .As required
12 Hatches/Harnesses/Passengers . . . . All secure

Hover

1 C of G . . . . Check
2 Torques . . . . Matched, N_R 385-39
3 Warning lights . . . . Out
4 Ts and Ps . . . . .Within limits

Cruise

1 Power . . . . .Max cont 73Q or 738 T4
2 Landing light . . . . Off
3 Fuel . . . . Checked
4 Ts and Ps . . . . .Within limits

Descent/Landing

1 Radios . . . . .Set
2 Landing light . . . . As required
3 Float pin . . . . As required
4 Altimeter . . . . Set
5 Fuel . . . . Balanced, contents
6 Engine anti-ice . . . . .As required

Shutdown

1 Collective . . . . Fully down
2 Controls . . . . Central, frictions on
3 Horn . . . . Off
3 Throttles . . . . GI, run for 2 mins
4 Electrics/Radios . . . . Check ELT, Off
5 Engine anti-ice . . . . Off
6 Horn, Pitot, Txfer, Gyros . . . . Off
7 Throttles . . . . Close after 2 mins (F1), observe TOT
8 Autorelight 1 & 2 . . . . Off
9 Generators/Boost pumps . . . . Off
10 Battery. . . . . Off when N1 = 0
11 Rotor Brake. . . . . Apply below 170 N_R, then fully Forward
12 Direct battery switches. . . . . Off

Picture: Cougar AS 355 in New Brunswick

EMERGENCIES

There are two types of emergency - those that require an autorotative landing, and those that don't. Those in this chapter are selected highlights from various flight manuals and tend to cover general concepts only, or have been developed from working practice - the proper manual should be checked for your machine.

Meanwhile...

LANDING URGENCY DEFINITIONS

A little common sense is involved here:

- **Land as Soon as Possible**. Land without delay at the nearest location at which a safe approach and landing is reasonably assured. Do not land in on somebody's barbecue when there is an empty field next door!

- **Land as Soon as Practicable**. Extended flight beyond the nearest approved landing area is not recommended. That is, land at the nearest airfield at which technical support is available (a maintenance facility). If none is reasonably close, land where the engineers can get to you later

EMERGENCY EQUIPMENT

Fire Extinguisher

This may be used on all fires.

Emergency Exits

Normal cabin doors which are jettisonable.

AUTOROTATIONS

Autorotative emergencies (engine failure, etc.) are dealt with under their own headings later - this bit discusses the autorotation process itself, assuming that the rotor RPM are correctly set - it would appear that many ships have them set too low because, when the FFCL is set for FLIGHT, the RRPM cannot go below the equivalent engine speed, and the engine is keeping the RRPM in the green rather than the airflow through the rotors. Check out Section 8 of the flight manual for the low pitch stop setting procedure.

65 kts (70 minus 1 knot per thousand feet for the B4) is recommended for the airspeed in autorotation, which must be held down to the flare height of 65 (70) feet*, because the speed you have at the flare affects blade inertia and the descent rate. In other words, do not bring the cyclic back as you begin to be affected by the sight picture when you get closer to the ground (Bell 206 pilots used to 60 knots of airspeed in autorotation take note). If you are prone to this, then come down at 70 kts, which is easier to maintain anyway as there is no marking on the ASI for 65 knots.

*The lower the flare, the longer is the run-on and the more rapid are control movements required. The Australian Defence Force determined that you need the least amount of collective at the landing phase with a flare height of 100 ft, so somewhere between 65 and 100 feet is good.

If the RRPM is set properly, you only need a little collective to keep the N_R in the green. This small amount should be reduced to zero when the flare is started to stop ballooning and give you that bit more during the touchdown.

Keeping the RRPM near the red line in a real emergency will also give you some more inertia. In training, of course, the yellow range is more appropriate.

You need to level when the tail is between 5 - 15 feet above the ground (it is around 30 feet behind you).

Tip: Try flying straight and level at autorotational speed at the proper height to get used to the sight picture.

If the aircraft is level on touchdown, it will accelerate because the rotor mast is tilted 3° forward, so you should touch down on the heels of the skids without dragging the stinger. Once on the ground, bring the cyclic slightly aft and lower the collective carefully to help with deceleration.

NON-AUTOROTATIVE EMERGENCIES

The general rule would be to tell ATC what is going on, and land at a suitable point.

Hydraulic System Failures

In general, with a hydraulic failure, the speed must be brought back to 60 knots, after which the switch on the collective lever should be actuated to ensure that all the accumulators are dumped at the same time (more information in the *Systems* chapter). The purpose of the accumulators is to allow you enough time to reduce speed from the cruise to 60 knots.

YAW SERVO CONTROL SLIDE VALVE FAILURE

Indicated by resistance to control movements.

- **In the hover**. If there is no movement about the yaw axis, land normally. If there is rotation about the yaw axis, cut off hydraulic pressure by actuating the switch on the collective lever.

- **In cruising flight**. Reduce speed, entering into a side-slip if necessary, then cut off hydraulic pressure by actuating the switch on the collective lever.

MAIN SERVO CONTROL SLIDE VALVE FAILURE

Actuate the switch on the collective lever to cut off hydraulic pressure. Load feedback will be felt immediately, and it may be heavy if the helicopter is flying at high speed. The control loads involved are:

- Collective pitch: 20 kg pitch increase load
- Cyclic: 7 - 4 kg left-hand cyclic load
- Cyclic: 2 - 4 kg forward cyclic load
- Yaw pedals: practically no load in cruising flight

Reduce speed to 60 knots (110 km/hr) and proceed as for illumination of the HYD light.

Governor Rundown

INDICATIONS

Rotor RPM decrease with low N_G and possible continuous audio warning.

IMMEDIATE ACTIONS

Lower collective and advance throttle forward of the flight gate. Raise the collective to establish acceptable N_R. Coordinate throttle & collective, land as soon as possible.

Governor Runup

INDICATIONS

Rotor RPM increase with high N_G and possible intermittent audio warning.

IMMEDIATE ACTIONS

Raise collective, close throttle slightly. Coordinate throttle and collective, land as soon as possible.

System Failures

FUEL FLOW RATE DROP

Symptoms are as for engine failure, with the exception that NG stabilises at a low rate (less than 70%) after a few seconds. When this happens, establish autorotation and advance the fuel flow control into the emergency sector. You should get a rise in N_G and T_4. Keep the engine speed at 70% and increase collective if necessary to bring the rotor speed to 350 RPM. Then increase the fuel flow till the rotors are running at 380 RPM - trim collective and fuel flow for level flight at this speed.

EXCESSIVE FUEL FLOW

Symptoms are increasing N_G, T_4 and Torque. Do not reduce collective but reduce fuel flow until rotor speed corresponds to a position of the indicator pointer in the centre of the green area. Continue flight with the governor out of action. If you reduce the collective, you will have to make a corresponding adjustment in the fuel flow as the RPM will increase. Make a low approach at 65 kts, holding the rotor at the upper limit of the green area (394 RPM) with the fuel flow control (you can leave it alone during finals, as the rotor speed will drop when you increase collective). After touchdown, reduce the fuel flow before decreasing collective.

SURGING

Symptoms are oscillations of RPM, Torque and T_4, and jerks in the yaw axis. The initial reaction should be to change the collective setting. If surging carries on while fuel and engine oil pressures are correct, reduce fuel flow slightly to take it out of the governed range. If you still get it, land as soon as possible and shut down.

ZERO FUEL PRESSURE

Check the fuel contents, and the booster pump. If the gauge reading is low, land immediately. If it is OK, check the gauge and pump fuses. If fuel pressure does not improve, land as soon as practicable, avoiding hot and high operations. Do not take off again with an inoperative fuel pump.

LOW FUEL PRESSURE

When the gauge starts reading in the yellow arc, test the **F FILT** caption. If it is working*, the filter is not clogged. Check the DC voltage - if it is normal, suspect the fuel pump or gauge. Land as soon as practicable.

*If it is not working, the fuel filter may be clogging.

LOW ENGINE OIL PRESSURE

There may be erratic torque indications, with the **ENG P** caption illuminating. Test the **ENG P** caption, check the torque gauge and reduce speed to 80 kts. If both are normal, the indication may be spurious, in which case land as soon as practicable. Otherwise, land as soon as possible. Consider an engine-off landing, or make a power-on landing where a successful one can be made.

HIGH ENGINE OIL TEMPERATURE

Engine oil temperature above 110°C. If in a prolonged hover with no other indications, transition into forward flight (at least 80 kts) and watch for a decrease. If temperature does not decrease, land as soon as possible.

In the cruise with no other abnormal indications, reduce speed to 80 kts. If temperature does not decrease, land as soon as possible.

The oil cooler fan should come on at 86°C and stop at 74°C as temp drops.

Indicator Failures

TORQUEMETER

Check the **ENG P** caption and the engine oil pressure gauge. Check the gauge fuse and do not exceed N_G chart values in the flight manual chart. In the hover, keep the helicopter heading into wind, keep yaw pedal movements to a minimum and avoid climbing turns to the right. If possible, carry out a minimum power landing. If a maximum torque power check was carried out on the first takeoff and the density altitude has not changed appreciably, use the values of T4 and N_G as limiting power settings

ENGINE COMPRESSOR RPM (N_G)

Do not exceed maximum torque, monitor T4 and land as soon as practicable. If a maximum torque power check was carried out on the first takeoff and the density altitude has not changed appreciably, use the torque and T4 values as limiting power settings.

T4

Do not exceed maximum torque or engine limitations. Land as soon as practicable. If a maximum torque power check was carried out on the first takeoff and the density altitude has not changed appreciably, use the torque and N_G values as limiting power settings.

ROTOR RPM (N_R)

Maintain torque above 20%, avoid autorotation and high disc loading. Land as soon as practicable.

TAIL ROTOR FAILURE

Depending on what has failed, this may or may not require an autorotation.

If throttle can be reduced, and collective increased, this would reduce the effect of the tail rotor at the same time as keeping the lift from the main rotors. The tail rotor is there to counteract torque, so if it is given less work to do, there will be more success. Tail thrust actually drops by something like the RPM^2, so 90% N_R means the tail rotor is down to 81% of max thrust (0.90 x 0.90). Also, main rotor torque goes up by the RPM drop, so the torque required to hover goes up by 10%, and more tail thrust is required to provide the anti-torque. This combination (tail thrust down and main torque up) is almost perfect to absorb max tail rotor angle.

Otherwise, there might be a power and speed combination that will maintain height until a suitable landing area is found, then there is as much time as the fuel lasts to solve the problem. The cyclic can be useful for changing direction and enabling sideways flight to create drag from the tail boom and vertical stabiliser, for example. It is the sort of situation where it pays to be creative - the aim is to walk away, not necessarily to preserve the machine. With a jammed power pedal, what also works is to crab in the way the machine wants to, come to a high hover sideways and let the machine settle by itself. Very little input is required by the pilot.

If a run-on landing is required, get the wind and/or nose off to the right, so the fuselage is crabbing, and control the (shallow) descent with collective. For a running landing, around 30% torque at 30 kts* will mean a good position for landing at 30 ft, and a little power at the last minute will put the nose nicely straight. For the non-power pedal, keeping straight involves either more speed or less power, and more run-on speed. Once on the ground, keep the collective in the same position as for the landing and shut down the engine. This removes the yaw and helps keep the machine straight.

*If the airspeed is lower than 20 kts, you will not be able to go around because the fin loses its efficiency.

Control Failure

- Set IAS 70 knots (130 km/hr), in level flight

- Press the hydraulic accumulator test push-button, which cuts off hydraulic power to the yaw servo control and depressurizes the load-compensating servo accumulator. After 5 seconds, reset the test button to the normal position

- Make a shallow approach to a clear landing area with a slight sideslip to the left and perform a run-on landing; the side slip will be reduced progressively as power is applied

Drive Failure

Loss of the tail rotor in power-on flight results in a yawing moment to the left. Its extent will depend on what power and speed you are using.

A drive failure, or loss of a component, will cause an uncontrollable yaw, and possibly an engine overspeed, so the immediate reaction should be to enter autorotation, keeping up forward speed to maintain some directional control, if there is time.

If a component is lost, the C of G will shift forward and reduce the aft cyclic available. Pilots who have been there report that there is a significant increase in noise with a drive shaft failure, and that the centrifugal force in the spin is quite severe. As speed is reduced towards touchdown, you will yaw progressively with less control available in proportion, so it may be worth trying to strike the ground with the tailskid first, which will help you to keep straight. Burn off the extra speed for best auto speed, stabilize, and make the landing.

In The Hover Or At Low Speed

IGE

Bring the aircraft to the ground by reducing collective before the yaw rate is too high.

OGE

Reduce collective moderately, to reduce the torque from the yaw, and simultaneously start to pick up speed.

© *Phil Croucher, 2011*

FIRE

During Start

INDICATIONS

FIRE

Possible smoke and flames

INTERNAL FIRE

1 Ventilate the engine for 10 seconds
2 Battery . . . . Off

COMPARTMENT FIRE

3 Throttle . . . . Close
4 Fuel shutoff . . . . Close
5 Fuel pump . . . . Off
6 Rotor Brake . . . . .Apply
7 Abandon aircraft with fire extinguisher
8 Warn passengers of rotating blades if applicable

In Flight

INDICATIONS

FIRE

Possible smoke and flames

IMMEDIATE ACTIONS

1 Passengers (and crew). . . . . .Warn
2 External Load . . . . Jettison
3 Throttle . . . . .Close
4 Fuel Pump. . . . . Off
5 Generator . . . . Off
6 Radio . . . . .Call MAYDAY
7 Floats (if over water). . . . . Inflate (should be armed already)
8 Battery . . . . Off if radio not required
9 Carry out engine-off landing
10 Rotor Brake. . . . . Apply
11 Abandon aircraft with fire extinguisher
12 Warn passengers of rotating blades if applicable

SMOKE IN THE CABIN

If you can identify where the smoke is coming from, shut down the offending system and use the fire extinguisher if necessary (it could be hydraulic fluid being pulled through the engine). Ventilate the cabin.

If you don't know where the smoke is coming from, turn off the heater. If that doesn't work, switch off the electrical master, then all systems, including the generator and alternator once the smoke has cleared. Reset the electrical master, and switch on the generator again, checking voltage and current. Switch systems back on, one by one, until problem is identified.

ENGINE FAILURE

Autorotation

The procedures for **practice autorotations** on the AS 350 depend on the model and are found in the appropriate flight manual. However, the general procedure is:

- Reduce collective pitch to establish autorotation configuration

- Monitor and control rotor RPM

- During final approach, shut down the engine, or reduce power, maintaining the N_G above 67%

- After touchdown, still at low collective pitch, apply the normal starting procedure

The procedure should result in a landing with either zero or partial engine power (i.e. 67% N_G). If you might need engine power for recovery, as in an overshoot, the FFCL should not be retarded from its normal flight position.

Hover IGE

INDICATIONS

GEN		ENG P

Audio . . . . Low speed horn
TOT, N_G, N_R . . . . Decreasing
Torque . . . . Zero
Yaw and Roll . . . . To the right

IMMEDIATE ACTIONS

1 Yaw . . . . Control
2 Collective. . . . . Raise, to cushion touchdown

SUBSEQUENT ACTIONS

3 Collective. . . . . Lower after touchdown
4 Throttle . . . . Close
5 Fuel Pump. . . . . Off
7 Generator . . . . Off
9 Battery . . . . Off

Hover OGE

INDICATIONS

GEN	ENG P

Audio . . . . Low speed horn
TOT, N_G, N_R . . . . Decreasing
Torque . . . . Zero
Yaw and Roll . . . . To the right

IMMEDIATE ACTIONS

1 Collective . . . . Lower Immediately
2 Cyclic. . . . . Apply for forward speed according to height
2 Yaw . . . . Control
Refer to B3.3.5.3

SUBSEQUENT ACTIONS

3 Collective . . . . Lower after touchdown
4 Throttle. . . . . Close
5 Fuel Pump. . . . . Off
7 Generator . . . . Off
9 Battery. . . . . Off

In Flight

INDICATIONS

GEN	ENG P

Audio . . . . Low speed horn
TOT, N_G, N_R . . . . Decreasing
Torque . . . . Zero
Yaw and Roll . . . . To the right

IMMEDIATE ACTIONS

1 Collective. . . . . .Lower immediately

. . . . Monitor & Control Rotor RPM

. . . . Min ROD speed 65 kts

2 Yaw, N_R . . . . Control

SUBSEQUENT ACTIONS

3 Passengers (and crew). . . . . Warn

4 External Load . . . . Jettison

5 Throttle . . . . .Close

6 Fuel Pump. . . . . Off

7 Fuel Shutoff Valve . . . . Off

8 Generator . . . . Off

9 Radio . . . . .Call MAYDAY

10 Floats (if over water). . . . . Inflate (should be armed already)

11 Battery . . . . Off if radio not required

12 Approach. . . . . Into Wind

13 At 65 ft, flare nose-up

14 At 20-25 ft, at constant attitude, apply collective to reduce sink rate

15 Level, cancel sideslip

16 Cushion landing with collective

Note: Do not inflate the floats over 5000' above the intended landing surface.

Engine Restarting In Flight

1 IAS. . . . . 65 kts

2 Height . . . . .Below 13,000 feet

3 N_G . . . . Below 30% to avoid jerks on resynchronisation

3 Throttle . . . . .Closed

4 Fuel Shutoff Lever . . . . .Open

5 Fuel Pump. . . . . .On

6 Starter Button . . . . Press

7 Treat as for engine start

© *Phil Croucher, 2011*

Engine Surge

Symptoms include large fluctuations of engine parameters - N_G may drop with rise in T4. There may also be associated hunting of the engine.

Reduce collective, and if surging persists, retard throttle lever out of governed band, and coordinate with collective. Land as soon as possible, consider engine-off if surging excessive. After landing, close throttle before lowering collective.

WARNING LIGHTS

The theory is that, if nothing is wrong, there is no need to bother the pilot, so warning lights are there to tell you of an abnormal operating situation.

When they exist, green and blue lights indicate correct operating conditions, or confirmation of them. For example, the compressor bleed valve is green (on the B2) to indicate that the valve is open.

Amber lights can mean abnormal conditions or the reduction in capability of a system. Red lights indicate a serious operating danger which must be reacted to immediately. Very serious dangers also have an aural warning.

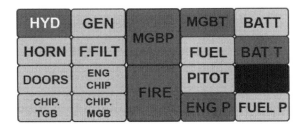

AS 350

These things almost never come on.

Light	Problem	Action
F Filt	Fuel Filter pre-clogging	Reduce power. If light goes out, continue at reduced power. Otherwise land ASAP
CHIP TGB	Metal in TGB	Continue, but avoid prolonged hovering (? - I think I would prefer to get on the ground as soon as possible. See 355 version)
CHIP MGB	Metal particles in MGB	Reduce power, monitor MGB.P and MGB.T lights. If either illuminate, refer to appropriate column
FUEL	Less than 15.8 US gals	If fuel is low, avoid large attitude changes. About 18 minutes' level flight at max continuous power
FUEL.P	Pressure lower than 2 bar, either or both pumps	If fuel pressure normal, one pump has failed, so continue. If zero, both have, keep below 5000 ft
FIRE	See above	
PITOT	Pitot system not energised	Check pushbutton, monitor ASI
HYD	Servo system failure	Do not depress HYD Test button - depressurises the accumulator. Calmly reduce collective and speed to between 40-60 kts. Cut off hydraulic press with button on collective. Make flat approach and land, slight forward speed
MGB.P	Main gearbox oil at min pressure	Reduce power, land ASAP
MGB.T	Main gearbox oil max temperature	Test caution panel to check light. If it does not come on, treat as oil pressure is zero. if it does, land and check oil level. You can fly to the nearest base if the level is normal
BAT T	Battery is at maximum temperature	Isolate the battery (pushbutton off) and land ASAP
ENG P	Engine oil pressure	Reduce power and check indicator. If pressure is low or 0, check torquemeter - shut down the engine if it is very low, and land immediately if it is normal. If pressure and torquemeter are normal, land ASAP

Light	Problem	Action
GEN	Either a DC supply failure or overvoltage has been detected	Test the DC voltage. Check the position of the pushbutton, then attempt to reset. If unsuccessful, loadshed and continue, ensuring you get at least 22 volts, and bearing in mind altitude limits when fuel booster pumps are off. Expect about 50 minutes from the battery by day, and 20 by night
BAT	Batt isolated from DC - not charging	Check the pushbutton (on) and keep an eye on the voltage
HORN	Horn not set	Actuate pushbutton on control pedestal panel
DOORS	One or both bge doors unlocked	Reduce airspeed to below 138 mph. Land carefully
ENG CHIP	Metal in engine oil	Land ASAP

AS 355

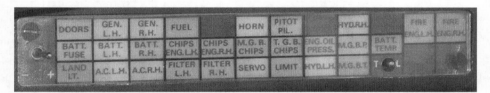

RED

System failures which require immediate action.

Item	Action
FIRE (LH or RH)	Excessive heat in relevant engine compartment. See 2.14.5
ENG P	Low engine oil pressure. Check gauge and torquemeter. Identify the affected engine, confirm within limits and shut it down
MGB P	Low gearbox oil pressure (<1 bar). If oil temperature or pressure out of limits, and/or **MGB T** caption is unserviceable, land as soon as possible
MGB T	Engine oil temperature above 155°C. If oil temperature or pressure out of limits, and/or **MGB P** caption is unserviceable, land asap
BATT T	Battery at maximum temperature. Switch off battery, land asap. Do not reselect battery if caption goes out

AMBER

Malfunctions which require no immediate action.

Item	Action
GEN LH or GEN RH	DC supply failed from whichever generator. If push button is in, push rearm button. If generator does not come online, switch it off and loadshed as necessary. Land as soon as practicable. If both lights come on, proceed as above, but also press Bus Shed button
BATT FUSE	Battery short circuit - not charging. Check for BATT T caption, check voltage. Do not switch of generators or shut down until back at a maintenance base
BATT LH or BATT RH	Battery contactor failure. Continue, and monitor loads. If both come on, batteries cutting out. Check that pushbuttons are engaged, and monitor BATT T caption. Monitor generators. Land as soon as practicable.

© *Phil Croucher, 2011*

Item	Action
CHIP LH or CHIP RH	Metal particles in engine oil. Monitor ENG P and temperature/pressure gauges. Shut down if other abnormal indications seen. If captions are out and indications within limits, land as soon as practicable. If one caption is on or one limit is reached, land as soon as possible.
TGB CHIP	Metal particles in TGB oil system. Land as soon as possible, allowing for tail rotor failure
SERVO	Main servo unit slide valve is jammed. Land as soon as practicable
LIMIT	Main servo unit at stall point because aerodynamic loads are excessive. Reduce collective and limit manoeuvres
HYD RH or HYD LH with SERVO	Loss of hydraulic pressure in relevant system. LIMIT light may also be on. Limit manoeuvres and land as soon as practicable
PITOT	No electrical supply to pitot heating system
DOORS	One or more baggage doors unlocked. Keep speed below 120 kts and land as soon as practicable, using shallow approach and avoiding high rate of descent
HORN	Horn alarm not set. Aural warning system may be defective
FILT LH or FILT RH	Fuel filter pre-clogged. Reduce power and continue if light goes out. If not, shut down affected engine. Possibly relight for landing. Do not transfer fuel unless absolutely necessary. If both come on, reduce power and land as soon as possible
FUEL	One gauge reads less than 6% contents. Avoid large attitude changes and balance tanks. Land before 10% total is remaining
AUTO R	Auto relight is on

WARNING AUDIO

Item	Action
Intermittent	N_R high - more than 410 RPM. Do not exceed 425 RPM on recovery
Continuous	N_R below 360 RPM

AS 355

• •

Double Engine Failure In The Hover

INDICATIONS

GEN	ENG P	AUTO R

Audio . . . . Low speed horn
TOT, N_G, N_R . . . . Decreasing
Torque . . . . Zero
Yaw and Roll . . . . To the right
RPM . . . . Possible Warning Lights and Audio

IMMEDIATE ACTIONS

1 Yaw . . . . Control
2 Collective. . . . . Raise, to cushion touchdown

SUBSEQUENT ACTIONS

3 Collective. . . . . Lower after touchdown
4 Throttles . . . . Close
5 Fuel Pumps . . . . Off
7 Generators . . . . Off
9 Battery . . . . Off

Double Engine Failure In Flight

INDICATIONS

GEN	ENG P	AUTO R

Audio . . . . Low speed horn

TOT, N_G, N_R . . . . Decreasing

Torque . . . . Zero

Yaw and Roll . . . . To the right

RPM . . . . Possible Warning Lights and Audio

IMMEDIATE ACTIONS

1 Collective . . . . .Lower immediately

. . . . Min ROD speed 65 kts

2 Yaw, N_R . . . . Control

SUBSEQUENT ACTIONS

3 Passengers (and crew) . . . . Warn

4 External Load . . . . Jettison

5 Throttles . . . . Close

6 Fuel shutoff levers . . . . Close

7 Fuel Pumps . . . . Off

8 Generators . . . . Off

9 Radio . . . . .Call MAYDAY

10 Floats (if over water) . . . . Inflate (max speed 61 kts - should be armed already)

11 Battery . . . . Off if radio not required

12 Carry out engine-off landing.

Note: Do not inflate the floats more than 5000' above the intended landing surface.

10

Engine Shutdown In Flight

1 Establish safe single-engined flight regime

2 Positively identify engine to be shutdown

3 Fuel Control Lever (throttle) . . . . Idle gate

. . . . Wait for two minutes if possible

4 Fuel Control Lever . . . . Close

5 Auto Relight . . . . Cancel caption

6 Fuel Shutoff Lever . . . . Close

7 Booster pump . . . . Off

8 Generator . . . . Off

9 Electrical loads on remaining generator . . . . .Monitor

Engine Restarting In Flight

1 IAS. . . . . Less than 100 kts

2 Height . . . . Above 2000 feet

3 Fuel Control Lever (throttle) . . . . Close

4 Fuel Shutoff Lever . . . . Open

5 Fuel Pump. . . . . On

6 Starter Button . . . . Press

7 Treat as for engine start

Single Engine Failure Before CDP (Clear Area)

INDICATIONS

GEN	ENG P	AUTO R

Audio . . . . Low speed horn
TOT, N_G, N_R . . . . Decreasing
Torque . . . . Zero
Yaw and Roll . . . . .To the right
RPM . . . . Possible Warning Lights and Audio

IMMEDIATE ACTIONS

1 Collective . . . . Adjust to retain height within limits
. .Decrease speed, set 15° nose up, increase pitch when aircraft sinks
2 Yaw, N_R . . . . Control

SUBSEQUENT ACTIONS

3 Collective . . . . Lower after cushioning touchdown
4 Throttle. . . . . .Close
5 Fuel Pump. . . . . Off
7 Generator . . . . Off
9 Battery. . . . . Off

Single Engine Failure Before CDP (Helipad)

INDICATIONS

GEN	ENG P	AUTO R

As for Clear Area, above

IMMEDIATE ACTIONS

1 Collective. . . . . .Lower to initiate descent back to helipad

2 N_R . . . . May be drooped to 375 if necessary

SUBSEQUENT ACTIONS

3 Collective. . . . . Lower after cushioning touchdown

4 Throttle . . . . .Close

5 Fuel Pump. . . . . Off

7 Generator . . . . Off

9 Battery. . . . . Off

Single Engine Failure After CDP (Clear Area)

INDICATIONS

GEN	ENG P	AUTO R

Audio . . . . Low speed horn

TOT, N_G, N_R . . . . Decreasing

Torque . . . . Zero

Yaw and Roll . . . . To the right

RPM . . . . Possible Warning Lights and Audio

IMMEDIATE ACTIONS

1 Speed . . . . Adjust to 40kts (V_{TOSS})

2 Collective . . . . Adjust to keep within limits

3 Fire . . . . Check for signs

SUBSEQUENT ACTIONS

4 Speed . . . . Adjust to 55kts (V_Y) after 550 feet

5 Failed engine . . . . Identify and shutdown:

6 Throttle . . . . Close

7 Fuel Pump . . . . Off

8 Generator . . . . Off

Single Engine Failure After CDP (Helipad)

INDICATIONS

GEN	ENG P	AUTO R

Audio . . . . Low speed horn
TOT, N_G, N_R . . . . Decreasing
Torque . . . . Zero
Yaw and Roll . . . . To the right
RPM . . . . Possible Warning Lights and Audio

IMMEDIATE ACTIONS

1 Nose . . . . Set 15° nose down
2 Collective . . . . Maintain 375 RPM

SUBSEQUENT ACTIONS

4 At 30 kts, reduce nose-down attitude
5 Speed . . . . Adjust to 40kts (V_{TOSS})
6 Collective . . . . Adjust to keep within limits
7 Fire . . . . Check for signs
8 Speed . . . . Adjust to 55kts (V_Y) after 550 feet
9 Failed engine . . . . Identify and shutdown:
10 Throttle . . . . Close
11 Fuel Pump . . . . Off
12 Generator . . . . Off

Single Engine Failure Before LDP (Landing)

INDICATIONS

GEN	ENG P	AUTO R

Audio . . . . Low speed horn

TOT, N_G, N_R . . . . Decreasing

Torque . . . . Zero

Yaw and Roll . . . . To the right

RPM . . . . Possible Warning Lights and Audio

IMMEDIATE ACTIONS

1 Attitude . . . . Flare to reduce speed close to ground

. . . . Level near the ground

2 Collective . . . . Increase to cushion landing

SUBSEQUENT ACTIONS

3 Collective . . . . Lower after landing

4 Failed engine . . . . Identify and shutdown:

5 Throttle . . . . Close

6 Fuel Pump . . . . Off

7 Generator . . . . Off

Single Engine Failure Before LDP (Going Around)

INDICATIONS

GEN	ENG P	AUTO R

Audio . . . . Low speed horn

TOT, N_G, N_R . . . . Decreasing

Torque . . . . Zero

Yaw and Roll . . . . To the right

RPM . . . . Possible Warning Lights and Audio

IMMEDIATE ACTIONS

1 Speed . . . . .Adjust to 40kts (V_{TOSS})

2 Collective. . . . . .Adjust to keep within limits

3 Fire . . . . .Check for signs

SUBSEQUENT ACTIONS

4 Speed . . . . Adjust to 55kts (V_Y) after 550 feet

5 Failed engine . . . . Identify and shutdown:

6 Throttle . . . . .Close

7 Fuel Pump. . . . . Off

8 Generator . . . . Off

9 Do not exceed 100 kts

Engine Fire During Start/On Ground

INDICATIONS

```
FIRE
```

Possible smoke and flames

INTERNAL FIRE

1 Ventilate the engine for 10 seconds
2 Battery. . . . . Off

COMPARTMENT FIRE

3 Emergency cutout . . . . Press
4 First fire extinguisher . . . . FIRE
5 Second fire extinguisher. . . . . .FIRE (if necessary)
6 Abandon aircraft with fire extinguisher
7 Warn passengers of rotating blades if applicable

Engine Fire In Flight

INDICATIONS

```
FIRE
```

Possible smoke and flames

IMMEDIATE ACTIONS

1 Reduce power and establish safe single-engined flight regime
2 Positively identify engine to be shutdown
3 Fuel Control Lever (throttle) . . . . Idle gate

If FIRE Caption Goes Out

4 Consider a hot gas leak, keep engine at idle for possible emergency use

If FIRE Caption Does Not Go Out

5 Fuel Shutoff . . . . Close

6 Booster pump . . . . Off

7 Bleeds . . . . Off

8 Radio . . . . Emergency Call

WHEN N$_G$ IS BELOW 50%

9 First extinguisher . . . . FIRE

10 Second extinguisher . . . . FIRE (if necessary)

If Fire Goes Out

11 Continue shutdown drills and land as soon as possible.

If Fire Not Out

12 Emergency Cutout . . . . Press

13 Fuel Shutoffs. . . . . .Close when on ground

14 Abandon aircraft with fire extinguisher

15 Warn passengers of rotating blades if applicable

Cabin Fire In Flight

Extinguish fire by best means, turn off heater and turn on all ventilation, providing that this does not fan the flames. Try to identify system involved and disable. Land as soon as possible.

Fire in MGB Compartment

Symptoms could include high engine or MGB oil temperature, and/or smoke and flames from the gearbox compartment.

Actions are to reduce power and land as soon as possible. If engie oil temperature exceeds 120°C, shut down engines.

Note: Fire in the MBG compartment may cause engine and MGB cooling system failure.

Frozen Fuel Flow

INDICATIONS

N_G, TQ and T4 on the affected engine do not change in response to collective movements.

IMMEDIATE ACTIONS

Keep affected engine within limits. If power is excessive, retard Fuel Control Lever to 40% TQ. Before lowering the collective fully for landing, select Ground Idle.

Runup or Rundown

INDICATIONS

N_G, TQ and T4 desynchronisation.

IMMEDIATE ACTIONS

Keep engines within limits. Lower collective to check for reductions in N_G, TQ and T4, keeping N_R within limits.

SUBSEQUENT ACTIONS

Retard Fuel Control Lever on the defective engine gently, checking for power response on the good engine. Set to 40% torque. Before lowering the collective fully for landing, select Ground Idle.

System Failures

STATIC SOURCE

Indicated by air instruments giving unreliable readings. Switch standby static source to STANDBY. Close all vents and windows. Reduce power, land as soon as practicable.

PITOT SOURCE

Indicated by lack of airspeed showing. Land as soon as practicable.

LOW FUEL PRESSURE

Check fuel contents, and that booster pumps are switched on. If a booster pump has failed, keep below 10,000 feet and land as soon as practicable.

HIGH OIL TEMPERATURE

Engine oil temperature above 107°C. If both engines are affected, land as soon as possible, and shut them down if they are above 120°C. If only one engine is affected, cross-check with the other engine and shut the affected engine down if necessary. Land as soon as practicable.

HIGH PEDAL LOADS

Where no captions are illuminated, the yaw servo unit slide valve is jammed. If in a stationary hover, land immediately and switch off the hydraulics (switch on the collective). In the cruise, reduce speed and switch off the hydraulics. If the pedal loading load remains, the failure is in the mechanical unit, so the hydraulics can be restored. Land as soon as practicable.

Indicator Failures

TORQUEMETER

Check the ENG P caption and the pressure gauge. Identify the affected engine, confirm within limits and shut it down. If readings are normal, equalise the T4s and do not exceed 65% on the good engine. Monitor all other parameters and land as soon as practicable.

ENGINE COMPRESSOR RPM (N_G)

Check that the affected engine is not malfunctioning, match the T4s and land as soon as practicable.

T4

Check that the affected engine is not malfunctioning, match the torques and land as soon as practicable. Do not exceed 700°C on the other engine.

QUESTIONS

11

These are the typical sort of questions you might find on a type rating test or technical exam.

AS 350

1. How is the FFC lever moved during startup?

2. When is the starter button released?

3. When do you activate the starter?

4. How do you isolate hydraulic pressure?

5. At what temperature must you add anti-icing additive to the fuel?

6. What is the minimum safe airspeed below 150 feet?

7. What is the minimum safe height for an OGE hover?

8. What are the starting limits into wind?

9. What is the V_{NE}?

10. What is the MAUW?

11. Where is the aft C of G at MAUW?

12. How much does V_{NE} reduce by per 1000 feet above 1000 feet DA?

13. What is the maximum normal operating speed?

14. What is the normal power on rotor speed in flight?

15. What is the maximum speed you can use the rotor brake?

16. What is the time limit between uses of the rotor brake?

17. At what RPM does the rotor low RPM audio sound?

18. What is the maximum torque limit?

19. What is the uphill slope limit?

20. What is the Ng transient limit in ISA conditions?#

21. What is the EGT transient limit on start up?

22. What is the EGT max continuous limit?

23. What is the minimum oil pressure?

24. What should the oil pressure be in flight?

25. What does the fuel warning light indicate?

26. What is the maximum oil temperature?

27. What are the maximum fuel contents?

28. What is the normal in-flight voltage?

29. What is the maximum amperage?

30. How are the rudder pedals adjusted?

31. Where is the friction for the cyclic control?

32. Where is the friction for the collective control?

33. Where are the spare fuses?

34. Where is the fuse for the instrument lights?

35. Where is the landing light switch?

36. Where is the rotor brake lever?

37. Is the fuel cock forward or backward when it is on?

38. What is the maximum floor loading in the rear floor of the cabin?

39. What is the maximum load in the starboard baggage hold?

40. Where is the battery?

41. Where is the external power socket?

42. How does the cyclic move when the hydraulics fail in flight?

43. How do you know the hydraulics have failed?

44. Which controls have hydraulic accumulators?

45. What is indicated if the BATT light comes on?

46. Which warning lights come on with external power connected prestart?

47. Where is the warning light panel?

48. What is the colour of the MGB.P light?

49. Where is the engine oil tank?

50. How do you check the contents of the engine oil tank?

51. Where is the hydraulic reservoir?

52. Where is the MGB sight glass?

53. Where is the torrque reading taken from?

54. How long is the rundown on the engine before stopping it?

55. What airspeed would you select if the hydraulics fail?

56. How much fuel is unusable?

57. How much engine oil should there be?

58. At what pressure does the hydraulic failure warning activate?

59. What is the battery capacity?

60. Where is the C of G datum point.

61. What Ng band should be avoided?

62. At what hydraulic pressure does the horn sound?

63. How much does the engine oil tank hold?

64. What is the minimum engine oil pressure in flight?

65. How many hydraulic servos are there?

66. What side of the hydraulic reservoir is the sight gauge on?

67. How is the hydraulic pump driven?

68. Does the hydraulic filter have a bypass?

69. Where is the pressure switch that activates the HYD light?

70. What does the hydraulic isolation switch or push button on the collective activate?

71. How do the accumulators provide hydraulic pressure after a hydraulic failure?

72. Which servo controls pitch?

73. When equipped with Dunlop servos which ones have a locking pin?

74. What are the B1 & B2 equipped with to assist with heavy tail rotor loads after a hydraulic failure?

75. Immediately after a hydraulic pressure failure what will be the control load on the cyclic?

76. What cockpit indication (s) is/are given after a hydraulic pressure failure?

77. What will you feel in the flight controls during a slide valve seizure?

15. What is the first action taken during a slide valve seizure?

AS 355

•••

F Models

1. What is the MAUW of the F1?

2. What is the V_{NE} (zero PA)?

3. What is the V_{NO} (zero PA)?

4. What is the V_{NE} with doors off?

5. What is the max RPM for rotor brake application?

6. What is the max continuous torque AEO?

7. What is the max continuous torque OEI?

8. What is the max transient torque OEI?

9. What is the max TOT, and for how long?

10. What is the max transient TOT, and for how long?

11. What is the max temperature for takeoff on 2 engines?

12. What is the max continuous temperature OEI?

13. At what temperature, in visible moisture conditions, should the engine anti-icing be switched on?

14. Where are the anti-icing system levers?

15. Below what temperature should you add a fuel anti-icing additive?

16. What is the minimum engine oil pressure?

17. What is the minimum MGB oil pressure?

18. What are the three types of restricted flight?

19. What are the slope limitations?

20. How is fuel transferred between the tanks?

21. Which engine does the forward fuel tank supply?

22. Where are the emergency fuel cutoff levers?

23. What would you notice if the left hand hydraulic pump failed?

24. What would you notice if the right hand hydraulic pump failed?

25. Where are the hydraulic reservoirs?

26. What actions are required if the LIMIT light comes on in flight?

27. How many heat exchangers service the main transmission?

28. Where are the oil coolers?

29. Where is the main transmission sight glass?

30. Where are the batteries?

31. What services would you expect to lose if the right hand generator fails?

32. What services would you expect to lose if one inverter fails?

33. Why should the cabin heating be selected off for takeoff and landing?

34. How is the windscreen wiper activated?

35. Why is there a spring steel strip at the rear end of each skid?

36. What is the max weight in the rear baggage locker?

37. What is the max weight in the port side baggage locker?

38. What is the max regulated voltage on the generator?

39. What is the max rated current of a generator, post mod AMS 156?

40. What is the MAUW for Category B operations?

41. What is the usual fuel consumption?

42. What is V_{TOSS}?

43. What is V_Y?

44. What is the minimum INC speed?

45. How high is the TDP for the helipad profile?

46. Can you mix mineral and synthetic engine oil?

47. What oil is used in the engines?

48. What chemical is used in the engine fire extinguishers?

49. Where is the C of G datum point?

50. What is the rearward C of G at 2400 kg?

51. What is the maximum Pressure Altitude for flight?

52. What should yo do if the GEN warning light comes on?

53. Which way does the yaw go if the tail rotor drive shaft goes?

54. What should you do if the BATT TEMP light comes on?

55. Can you start both engines from one battery on an IFR machine?

56. What should you do if the FILTER light comes on in flight?

57. What action is needed if the Tq gauge fluctuates?

58. What is the maximum torque for an AEO takeoff?

59. What is the max continuous AEO torque?

60. What is the max continuous OEI torque?

61. What is the max continuous AEO T4?

62. What is the max engine oil temperature?

63. At what level does the fuel flow light come on?

64. How is VHF Comm 1 powered?

65. What are the max contents of the forward fuel tank?

66. What are the max contents of the rear fuel tank?

67. What engine does the rear fuel tank feed?

68. If a fuel gauge float valve jams, does the low fuel warning light come on?

69. Where are the direct battery fuses?

70. Where are the voltmeters?

71. Which system powers the tail rotor servo?

72. At high pitch, what CWP warning do you get for RH hydraulic failure?

73. What CWP lights indicate a hydraulic selector valve jam?

74. What is the function of the HYD switch on the collective?

75. Where is the main gearbox temperature sensor?

76. How is main rotor gearbox oil cooled?#

77. How do the main rotor blades flap up?

78. How is main rotor RPM detected?

79. When does the horn sound for rotor problems?

80. How are the tail rotor pedals linked to the tail rotor servo?

81. How is the friction on the collective lever adjusted?

82. How are the engines balanced?

83. Where is the freewheel for No 1 engine?

84. What types of gears are in the main gearbox?

85. Which busbar would you lose if the RH generator fails?

86. What does the emergency cutoff switch do?

Picture courtesy Great Slave Helicopters

ANSWERS

These are the answers......

AS 350

1. As soon as the starter is pressed, move it to mid-range.

2. Between 40-45%.

3. 30 seconds after putting on the boost pump.

4. Press the button on the end of the collective.

5. 0°C.

6. 60 kts.

7. 800 ft.

8. 48 kts.

9. 147 kts.

10. 1950 kgs.

11. 3.43.

12. 3.5 kts.

13. 10 kts below calculated V_{NE}.

14. 380-386 RPM.

15. 170 RPM.

16. 5 minutes.

17. 335.

18. 83%.

19. 10°.

20. 105%.

21. 840°.

22. 775°.

23. 1.9 bar.

24. 3.2 - 9 bar.

25. The contents are below 60 litres.

26. 110°C.

27. 116 Imp Gals (418 kg).

28. 26-29 V.

29. 150 amps.

30. There is a two-position adjustment.

31. There is a knurled wheel around the base of the cyclic.

32. There is a sleeve on the collective lever.

33. In a panel just forward of the pilot's door.

34. On the panel along the right hand side of the console.

35. On the switch panel on the console.

36. On the left of the control quadrant between the seats.

37. Forward.

38. 310 kg.

39. 100 kg.

40. In the rear of the right hand baggage hold.

41. Just above the right hand rear cross tube mount.

42. To the rear and right.

43. There is a light on the warning panel, and a horn.

44. Cyclic and collective.

45. The battery is disconnected from the DC supply.

46. HYD, GEN, MGB.P, ENG.P, BATT.

47. On the top right hand side of the instrument panel.

48. Red.

49. On the right hand rear side of the transmission deck.

50. Observing the level through the translucent container.

51. Above the main drive shaft aft of the gearbox.

52. On the left hand side.

53. The engine.

54. 30 seconds.

55. 40-60 kts.

56. 8.7 kg.

57. 5.2 litres.

58. When pressure falls below30 bar.

59. 24v 16 A/H.

60. 3.4 m forward of the rotor mast centre.

61. 94-96%.

62. Less than 30 bar.

63. 5.2 litres (1.14 Imp gals).

64. 1.9 bar.

65. Four.

66. The right.

67. It is belt driven off of the MGB engine drive shaft.

68. No.

69. On the hydraulic distribution block.

70. The isolation solenoid valves on the main servos.

71. Expansion of the nitrogen filled bladder expels hydraulic fluid out of the accumulator.

72. Forward/left.

73. Pitch only.

74. A yaw load compensator.

75. Normal.

76. HYD light & horn.

77. An uncommanded control movement.

78. Disengage hydraulic system with isolation switch on collective.

AS 355

● ●

F Models

1. 2400 kg.

2. 150 kts.

3. 135 kts.

4. 70 kts.

5. 170.

6. 73%.

7. 100%.

8. 112% for 16 seconds.

9. 927° for 1 second.

10. 899° for 12 seconds.

11. 810°.

12. 810°.

13. 5°C.

14. Between the seats on the cabin floor.

15. 4°C.

16. 3.5 bar.

17. 1 bar (there is a red warning light).

18. Aerobatics, flight in icing conditions, Complete intentional autorotations.

19. Nose up 10°, Nose down 6°, Sideways 8°.

20. A combination of electro valve and gravity.

21. The left (No 1).

22. On the overhead panel, at the extreme left and right, wire locked.

23. The HYD amber light would come on, but there would be no effect on the servo system.

24. The HYD amber light would come on, but the pedal load would increase.

25. Behind the main rotor gearbox.

26. reduce the manoeuvre and pitch.

27. 2.

28. Between the oil filter and heat exchangers.

29. Near the combiner gearbox.

30. On the starboard side.

31. None.

32. The other one should be able to cope with both systems.

33. Because compressed air is taken from compressor.

34. By an overhead panel button and a switch under the collective.

35. To prevent ground resonance.

36. 80 kg.

37. 120 kg.

38. 28.5 volts.

39. 150 amps.

40. 2400 kg.

41. 30% per hour.

42. 40 kts.

43. 55 kts.

44. 55 kts.

45. 90 feet.

46. No.

47. MIL L 23699.

48. Freon.

49. 3.4 m forward of the main rotor head centre line.

50. 3.48 m.

51. 16 000 feet.

52. Check the amperage on the good generator, attempt to reset GEN.

53. Left.

54. Switch off the batteries.

55. No.

56. Reduce the fuel flow or shut down the engine.

57. Monitor engine oil pressure. Shut down the engine if it falls.

58. 78%.

59. 73%

60. 100%.

61. 738°C.

62. 107°C.

63. 6% in either tank.

64. Both systems.

65. 45%.

66. 55%.

67. No. 2 (right).

68. No.

69. Below the collective lever.

70. In front of the fuel flow levers.

71. The right hand one.

72. HYD RH + SERVO.

73. SERVO.

74. To switch off the tail rotor system.

75. On the port side base of the gearbox.

76. Through a matrix on both engine oil cooler systems.

© *Phil Croucher, 2011*

77. The starflex bends.

78. A phonic wheel and magnetic sensor.

79. Low or high rotor RPM.

80. By rod and flexible control.

81. By a controll at the base of the collective.

82. With a rocker switch on the collective lever.

83. In the combining gearbox.

84. Epicyclic and bevel.

85. The right hand one.

86. Cuts off both primary busbars.

Picture: View through the front panel with a sling load

INDEX